D0178016

© 1979 Norman Thelwell

.thelwell.

this book belongs to

Joanne Lennox

With special thanks to Sandra Pilcher

ACKNOWLEDGEMENTS

The author and publishers wish to thank the following for use
of colour transparencies and black-and-white photographs
appearing in the book: Kilverstone Wildlife Park; London Zoo;
Zoo Park, Twycross; Manor House Wildlife and Leisure Park;
Bristol, Clifton and West of England Zoological Society; The
Zoological Society of Glasgow and West of Scotland; Knowsley
Safari Park; Blackpool Municipal Zoological Gardens; Windsor
Safari Park; The Royal Zoological Society of Scotland, Edinburgh;
Banham Zoo; Jersey Wildlife Preservation Trust; The Zoological
Society of Wales; Chessington World of Adventure; Marwell
Zoological Park; Drusilla's Zoo Park; The Tropical Bird
Gardens, Rode; Linton Zoological Gardens; Thrigby Hall Wildlife
Gardens; Dartmoor Wildlife Park.

First published in 1988 by Planet Books,
a division of W. H. Allen & Co Plc

Typeset in Century by Input Typesetting Ltd, London
Printed by Scotprint Ltd, Musselburgh,
bound in Great Britain by Hunter & Foulis Ltd, Edinburgh
for the publishers W. H. Allen & Co Plc,
44 Hill Street, London W1X 8LB

Designed by Osborn & Stephens

ISBN: 1–85227–095–0

Cover picture: *A five-week-old, young male Indian tiger.*
Bruce Coleman Limited (Rod Williams)

Contents

Foreword   5
A Kinkajoo Called Jou-Jou   7
The Puzzle of the Giant Panda   10
The Thoughts of Johnny Chimp   13
Granny, the Squirrel Monkey   17
Sweetheart – The Tipsy Tawny Eagle   20
Jeremiah – A Terror of a Toddler   23
An Elephant Called Jubilee   27
A Tale of Two Tigers   29
The Loneliness of the Long-Distance Crane Keeper   32
George and his State Registered Rhino Nurse   35
Camel Carnival   38
Merlin the Mynah, and Other Precious Species   42
Morning Inspection   44
The New Arrivals   46
Penguins on Parade   49
There's no Leopards like Snow Leopards   52
A Life Full of Otters   55
Jambo – the Gentle Giant of Jersey   57
The Saga of Saga   61
Pringle – A Star is Born   65
Sire Basil – The Noblest of Stallions   69
Beavering Away   72
Three-Foot Flying Rainbows   76
Quasimodo Gets His Esmeralda   78
Breakfast at Timothy's   81
My Blunders with Black Basil   84
See the Sea-lions   87
What an Otter!   90
A Cat-alogue of Cat-astrophes   93
Zoo Addresses   96

A Kinkajoo Called Jou-Jou

KILVERSTONE WILDLIFE PARK

'A what-a-joo?'

'Kinkajoo—related to the olingo.'

That piece of information never fails to change an initially blank expression into one of complete bewilderment! All the visitor knows is that he has before him an adorable, furry baby with enormous eyes and a gorgeous expression.

To set the record straight, the kinkajoo is part of the Procyonidae family and is sometimes known as the honey bear. Kinkajoos have lovely thick fur, large round eyes, indicative of their nocturnal habits, and small rounded ears. They are about fifty centimetres long, excluding the long prehensile tail which approximately doubles their length. They are wonderful climbers and spend most of their time high in the trees of rain forests in Mexico and Brazil. They are classed as carnivores and will eat small birds and frogs, although their main diet consists of fruit. The first kinkajoo I hand-reared was Jou-Jou. She was brought into the house by a keeper, who, as I always instruct them when carrying newly-born babies, had 'stuck it up his jumper'! There is no better way to keep an animal warm, and being held next to a beating heart is very reassuring for a frightened baby. Jou-Jou had been taken away from her mother because she had killed her three previous babies.

Jou-Jou survived splendidly under my care and protection, although at first no one, not even my own children, could understand how I could be so attached to the ugly-looking creature. For the first ten days of a kinkajoo's life, it looks like a tiny, blind rat. By the eleventh day, however, Jou-Jou was miraculously transformed. Her eyes opened, wide and round, and all of a sudden the 'ughs' and 'arghs' her appearance had initially evoked turned into 'oohs' and 'aahs'.

All the animals that I hand-rear live at my house, as they require constant care and attention. By the time Jou-Jou was four months old, she had to share the kitchen with two of my other babies, Freddy, a tree-climbing fox, and Grumble, a jaguar cub. They were great friends and spent hours playing together, their games being mainly restricted to the kitchen, but if they ever got the chance, they would gambol and fight through the entire house. I tried to

Left: *Kinkajoos have lovely thick fur, large round eyes, indicative of their nocturnal habits, and small rounded ears.*

restrict these romps, particularly when the three of them ventured in the direction of the library. For Jou-Jou and Freddy, already being brilliantly adept climbers, the book-lined shelves, running from floor to ceiling, provided a wonderful challenge. Scaling the shelves, and systematically emptying them to make room for their chase, was tremendously exciting! Meanwhile, Grumble, whose climbing skills had yet to develop, would attempt to join in, but his fat and floppy milk tummy tied him to the ground. However, he contributed to the mayhem by completely destroying the lower shelves in his frustrated attempts to join the others!

At first I used to worry how poor little Jou-Jou would fare against her much larger playmates, but actually she always had the upper hand, squirming out of the tightest wrestling holds and using her ultimately versatile tail successfully to 'strangle' her opponents into submission. The older she became, the more nocturnal was her behaviour. When Freddy and Grumble were old enough to return to the park, Jou-Jou spent more and more of her time during the day wrapped up in a blanket. However, she would always be awake to greet me affectionately in the morning. She climbed up my arms to lick me all over the face and neck, then clasped me tightly while rubbing her head backwards and forwards under my chin. After holidays, during which I might be away for several weeks, this peculiar greeting could go on for ages, she was so delighted to see me.

The wonderful greeting was usually followed by a tour of inspection of the kitchen, which then had to be rearranged according to Jou-Jou's tastes. (Once I had been lax enough to leave her favourite cupboard open. She had a marvellous time with the pans and dishes, and managed to sound like a whole percussion band on her own.) The inspection complete—eggs duly broken, sugar spilt and butter paddled in—Jou-Jou would climb exhausted on to my husband, wiggle inside his jacket and curl up down one sleeve, so making it virtually impossible for him to eat his breakfast.

One morning, however, I discovered the kitchen window open and Jou-Jou nowhere in sight. Panic-stricken, I began searching the house. Suddenly, one of our staff who had a flat in the house appeared trembling, white and shaken. She had just got up to discover that there had been burglars in the night and they had completely wrecked her living-room. Some burglars! You did not have to be a detective to know that two and two make kinkajoo!

Jou-Jou remained with us in the house until she was three years old, when the time came for her to meet a male kinkajoo. My husband had just finished building the new nocturnal house, and my kinkajoo 'dating' service had provided a handsome boyfriend. So it was appropriate that Jou-Jou should be moved to new accommodation. Despite my exertions to provide her with the perfect arranged marriage, at first Jou-Jou despised her betrothed and bullied him dreadfully. When I visited her, she demanded my attention and insisted on cuddles. It was heart-breaking at times. Only eventually did she settle down with her henpecked husband, and redirect her affections.

When Jou-Jou started to spread around the middle, I was particularly delighted. It is the specific aim of Kilverstone to breed South American animals, especially those whose natural habitat and, therefore, existence are threatened. Jou-Jou's acceptance of 'married' life was a great relief, as she was the first kinkajoo that I had hand-reared, and I was frightened that she might have become too humanised. When she gave birth, Jou-Jou wanted her husband out of the way and told him so, in no uncertain tones. The keepers responded immediately and put the poor battered husband into a separate enclosure.

Alone, Jou-Jou settled down to nurse her new baby. Hubby, meanwhile, looked greatly relieved to be away from his wife! Baby spent most of its time curled up on Jou-Jou's tummy, sleeping and feeding in the warmth and confidence of its mother's protection. When the baby was four or five weeks old, the keepers suggested we should re-introduce the male. After a great deal of debate and argument, we did so, but under very close supervision. Unfortunately, Jou-Jou did not agree with the keepers, and flew at her estranged mate, almost killing him in her temper. The baby had been left on a high ledge while they fought and, during the excitement, it fell fatally to the ground.

I rushed to Jou-Jou. I knew how she had loved the baby and how proud of it she was. I thought she might be very upset —or was I imposing human emotions on the situation? Many animals seem totally unconcerned when an offspring dies. Whatever I envisaged, I was totally unprepared for her actual reaction. I opened the door of the house and said, 'My poor, poor Jou-Jou'. She picked up the dead baby in her mouth and carried it along the big log which lay diagonally across her room, crying all the way. Then she gazed up at me as if begging me to make it better.

My vision blurred as my eyes filled with tears. All I could hear were her cries of pain and distress. Closing the door behind me, I sat down and wept for her. I had to get the keeper to remove the baby, but she would not let it go—as if hoping it would suddenly get better or I could make it come back to life.

After a couple of weeks, the male was put back with her. She accepted him and life went on as before with them both sleeping on the high shelf. As Jou-Jou and her mate settled down together, she seemed to grow less fond of me— I had let her down and had not brought her baby to life. We had failed to mend it. Her implicit trust in us seemed to fade.

The Puzzle of the Giant Panda

THE ZOOLOGICAL SOCIETY OF LONDON

'Heineken refreshes the parts that other pandas can't reach', read the optimistic advertising slogan before Chia Chia's famous transatlantic mission to Washington Zoo. The poster bore the picture of London Zoo's most famous resident, whose forthcoming journey to meet the American zoo's female panda had created massive media interest. He found himself at the centre of a world-wide press campaign, featuring on the front page of newspapers and as a main item on radio and television news programmes.

The importance of the trip was recognised by everybody. The giant panda, being the emblem of the World Wildlife Fund, symbolises the whole problem of conservation and the need to breed the species is universally understood. There are only twenty pandas outside China and altogether probably less than a thousand left in the wild. So when Washington's male showed no interest in his mate, the zoo's staff decided to see if they could arrange for her to meet another male. The zoo's 'international dating network' sprang into action and quickly discovered that Chia Chia was certainly very interested in the opposite sex but, sadly, had not been able to produce any offspring with his mate Ching Ching. Perhaps Chia Chia would be just the panda Washington was looking for!

So, elaborate plans were made for Chia Chia's American vacation. A blaze of publicity surrounded the historic flight. Never had one animal received such adulation. Chia Chia, being the only giant panda in Britain, was quite used to the celebrity treatment and so took it all in his stride. He retained his naturally placid and friendly disposition and was totally unaffected by the attention he received! He was not the first panda from London Zoo to be flown thousands of miles in order to help maintain the numbers of the species. His predecessor, An An, had helped lift the Iron Curtain a few inches when he made a famous visit to Moscow Zoo.

Sadly, in both cases, the travelling was to no avail. In fact, Chia Chia let the side down completely. He simply did not fancy his 'bride-to-be', and he let his feelings be known in no uncertain terms by attacking the poor female who had

Above: *The giant panda is the emblem of the World Wildlife Fund, as it symbolises the whole problem of conservation. There are only twenty pandas outside China, and probably less than a thousand left in the wild.*

waited so long to meet her suitor. Not surprisingly, his ignominious return journey did not gain the same interest as his outward trip. Poor Chia Chia was cast as a failure by the very advertising and media men who had built up his reputation as a superstud in the first instance. But, as the saying goes, revenge is sweet.

A few years later, Chia Chia proved them all wrong. A baby male panda, Chu Lin, was born in Madrid Zoo—his father was none other than Chia Chia! This time, however, the parents did not actually meet, as the mother was artificially inseminated, and thus the possibility of a repeat performance of the American adventure was eliminated.

It is not so surprising that it has proved difficult to breed pandas in captivity as, even in the wild, the chances of successfully producing a baby panda are slim. Pandas live solitary lives, often separated from one another by hundreds of miles. As the female is only able to conceive during four days of the year, it is crucial that there is a male nearby at that specific time. If not, it is a long, long wait until the next time she will be able to have a baby.

Pandas are equally particular about their diet. Chia Chia would need to eat twenty-five kilos of bamboo a day in the wild. While in the zoo, his diet is supplemented with rice, honey, eggs, mincemeat and special pellets containing vitamins. But he still requires a great deal of bamboo which is not normally grown in Britain. Being such a celebrated animal, however, Chia Chia has a very special source of bamboo. The bulk of his supply is provided by the efforts of the Polkerris Boy Scout troop from Cornwall, who gather the bamboo for the zoo and send it by Red Star to London every day. In return for their remarkable efforts and reliability they are the only scout troop allowed to wear the special panda insignia, as a reward for the contribution to the welfare of the giant panda.

Perhaps the only demonstration of his recognition of his much vaunted position in the animal world is Chia Chia's fickleness over food. While in the USA, he developed a passion for the large Washington Red apples. Yet all the time he had been at London Zoo, he absolutely refused to eat any fruit and appeared particularly to dislike apples. His British keepers remained quite sceptical about his newly discovered taste and so, to prove a point, the American keeper who accompanied Chia Chia on his journey home brought with her a whole crate of these special apples.

On American soil, right up to the point when he was ready to be transported, Chia Chia munched happily and eagerly on the juicy, red fruit. When he eventually arrived in London, the keeper once again offered him an apple. He sniffed at it and then rejected it. At first, the American keeper thought that he was probably suffering from a panda version of jet lag and just did not fancy his favourite titbit at that particular time. So she left the crate, convinced that once he had settled down again, he would continue to enjoy his American treat.

But no. Try as they might, the British keepers could never persuade Chia Chia to eat an apple again. To this day, he completely refuses even to consider the fruit—no matter how red or juicy!

The Chinese are, quite correctly, very protective of their special bear, which is only presented to heads of state very occasionally. Chia Chia and Ching Ching were presented to Edward Heath in 1974, and similar pairs were given to President Nixon at the same time. The problem facing western zoos at the moment is that there is now a surplus of males, and no females with which to breed. Constant research is being carried out, however, and the Zoological Society of London and the World Wildlife Fund have helped the Chinese Government to set up the research centre at Wolong, while invaluable work is being carried out at the London Zoo research centre itself, in order to understand better the reproductive cycle of the panda and therefore to assist the preservation of the species. And so Chia Chia, as well as being the 'superstar' of London Zoo, may help to solve the puzzle of the giant panda.

The Thoughts of Johnny Chimp

ZOO PARK, TWYCROSS

n exclusive interview with Johnny Chimp by Malcolm Whitebread, the director of education at Twycross Zoo

Johnny is, arguably, Britain's most famous chimpanzee. He lives at Twycross Zoo in the Midlands, where he has been a resident for twenty-five years. Now a grey-haired and venerable member of a celebrated group of chimps, his memory stretches back to the days of his youth when he lived in a rain forest in West Africa. In this exclusive conversation, Johnny reflects upon his life and times.

M. W.—*So Johnny, what's it like being a common chimpanzee in the 1980s?*
Johnny Chimp—Chimps are not common. Our manners and customs are highly sophisticated. Chimpanzees are being hounded in all parts of their wild habitat—whether it's a case of losing our native forests or being hunted for food or trade. There are about two hundred thousand of us left in the wild in some fifteen African countries.

M. W.—*Tell us about the old country.*
Johnny Chimp—I was born in a rain forest in West Africa. Some of the trees are seven or eight times taller than a giraffe, and they are organised into separate layers or storeys—rather like your blocks of flats. Just to experience the whistling contact calls of the brightly patterned Diana monkeys, the clamorous chatter of a bevy of hornbills, and the solitary elegance of the bongo antelope is wonderful. Of course, a lot of forest has disappeared. Loggers destroyed it. Just a charred, burnt-out desert these days.

M. W.—*Tell me, Johnny, did you live in the forest with your family?*
Johnny Chimp—Yes—and with others. Chimps certainly know about extended families. There were eighty of us. My mum and I used to belong to an ape-like version of a mother and toddler group and my dad was always out with the lads. When one or two of the smaller groups got together it was mayhem.

Pant hooting, breaking sticks, displaying. What a laugh! Mum was always strict about one thing. You did not mix with chimps from neighbouring families. If you stepped outside your own territory you had to watch out. I heard stories about gangs of adolescent males wandering into neighbouring territories for aggressive raids and a spot of mischief. Hooligans!

M. W.—So, how come you ended up at Twycross?
Johnny Chimp—It's a rather complicated story. Something happened to my mum and I was picked up by Africans and handed over to a white man who had several other baby chimps. We were all put on a boat to England and after several weeks we arrived in London. I was sold to a farmer who soon got tired of my boyish pranks. My big white chief heard of my plight and came and rescued me. He then took me to Twycross Zoo.

M. W.—Does this sort of thing still go on—taking chimps from the wild?
Johnny Chimp—Not in responsible zoos. There is no need to. Chimps breed well in captivity these days. Twycross even keeps stud books of all the chimps and gibbons living in British zoos.

M. W.—So, no chimps are taken from the wild?
Johnny Chimp—I didn't say that. I was talking about zoos. There are still chimps being taken from the wild. For example, all those baby chimps on the Costa Brava. They are exploited by unscrupulous photographers who traipse them round the clubs, bars and beaches for tourists to have their photographs taken with.

M. W.—What's wrong with that?
Johnny Chimp—For every chimp that reaches Spain or Tenerife, many die. Baby chimps are obtained by shooting their mothers. Some die in transit or at holding stations. In Spain, they're often drugged or murdered after a few short tourist seasons. And that's not to mention the chimps taken from the wild for biomedical research.

M. W.—But you are cosseted these days.
Johnny Chimp—Yes, Twycross Zoo is OK. Regular meals, good variety. First-class quality fruits, vegetables, seeds, bread, eggs and vitamins, as well as a few pints of blackcurrant juice. My main keeper, Dorothy, has been with me since the beginning. She's great.

M. W.—I understand that in your youth you were a very famous TV star?
Johnny Chimp—That is true. I appeared in lots of tea commercials and became

Right: *The chimpanzees at Twycross are famous for the appearances they have made in tea commercials on television.*

14

addicted to tea. I worked with great actors and actresses and always had my star dressing room. I loved travelling and stayed in five-star hotels. I really missed all this when I retired.

M. W.—*What about your friends?*
Johnny Chimp—Well, most of the time I live with Sam. He's also in his thirties and a TV star. Sam can out-display anyone when he stomps his feet and claps his hands. Coco is in her mid-twenties and came to Twycross from the Senegalese Army in 1969. She's very unusual—one of only two captive chimps (the other's her son, Jambo) that are brown rather than black. There is a young lad called Flynn around at the moment. He is twelve months old and behaves just like I did at his age. He gets lots of attention from visitors. Then there is Old Bimbo who is a volatile sort of chap and Chopper who tends to go a bit crazy from time to time. It gets rather like *EastEnders*. Some of us watch soap operas. Twycross Zoo's new chimp house, opened in 1982, is fully equipped with a colour TV. My chimp pals love watching horse racing, boxing and other wildlife programmes.

M. W.—*Are humans like chimps?*
Johnny Chimp—No, you walk upright all the time. You don't walk on your knuckles. You describe others as chinless wonders yet you have prominent chins. What you don't have is a good forehead—all normal great apes have a good brow ridge. Also, humans are so miserable. For years, I thought that you all went around in a perpetual state of fear. Then I realised that humans smile and show their teeth when they're happy. We do it when we are frightened. But we have many things in common. We live in family groups. We also quarrel occasionally with our neighbours—sometimes our keepers act as foster mums. Of course, you know more about us these days. In the 1950s, you thought we were peaceful, small-group-living, fruit-eating creatures. Since Jane Goodall, an honorary chimp, started studying us in the sixties, you've learned that our small groups are part of much larger ones. You know now that we occasionally eat meat, sometimes even killing monkeys or antelope and sharing the spoils in tribal fashion. You even know that we use tools: sticks and stone as weapons or for crushing hard fruits; twigs to fish for termites; and chewed leaves as sponges. A few years ago someone wrote a book called *Chimpanzee Politics*. At least you're beginning to realise that we're more complex than you thought!

Granny, the Squirrel Monkey

GATWICK ZOO AND AVIARIES

A t some time or another, every zoo has been approached by a member of the public who has unwisely chosen an exotic animal as a pet, only to discover that, no matter how kindly treated, it will never respond like a domestic cat or dog. Monkeys are particularly popular 'pets' and invariably prove to be too much to handle when they reach maturity and begin to display naturally aggressive behaviour. The sweet, cuddly baby, which was such enormous fun and a member of the family, suddenly turns into a dangerous beast prone to 'bite the hand that feeds it'. Often, kindness itself harms the animal. Exotic creatures require specialised diets and attention. A menu of chocolate, chips and hamburgers only results in a poor, ill creature.

Such was the case when Terry Thorpe of Gatwick Zoo was telephoned by a man about the future welfare of a squirrel monkey. Terry invited him to bring the animal to the zoo the following day.

The man arrived carrying a cardboard box under his arm. Terry asked about the animal's background. It turned out that the monkey had been the man's mother's pet, to which she had been devoted for many years. Sadly, his mother had recently died and had requested in her will that a good home be found for her beloved pet or that he be put to sleep humanely.

Gingerly Terry opened the lid of the box to peer inside. There, shivering in the corner was indeed a monkey, but to identify it as any particular species was almost impossible! All he could see was a mass of wrinkled, pink skin totally without fur! Worse still, the poor animal's limbs were swollen with rheumatism, making it appear deformed.

Terry had always considered the squirrel monkey one of the most beautiful of the primate family. Indeed, Gatwick Zoo has a magnificent group of squirrel monkeys which have bred successfully for years. The prospect of including this naked monkey in the group presented him with many problems—not least of which was the reaction of the public. Terry knew that visitors to Gatwick would quite rightly be shocked by the monkey's condition and no doubt would complain. Without knowing its history, the visitors were sure to think that Gatwick Zoo was responsible for its dreadful appearance. And yet, Terry could not bear to have the animal put down simply because it was old, ugly, and unwanted.

The solution was a compromise. Introducing a new animal into an existing, established group of monkeys is a delicate operation. Each group has a rigid structure and a newcomer has to find its correct place within the hierarchy. This task is fearsome even for a healthy animal; for such a sickly-looking creature, the struggle could be disastrous. So Terry decided that he would see whether the old monkey would be accepted by the others before agreeing to accept it permanently.

As he walked out into the zoo with the cardboard box, the other monkeys, inquisitive as ever, followed in the trees above. They were eager to examine the contents of the mysterious box. Terry found a suitable low branch and cautiously opened the lid. He then walked far enough away to observe the natural reactions of the group, but near enough to save the old monkey should it prove necessary. As the monkey slowly emerged from the box, all pink, wrinkled and bent, its new name became obvious to Terry—it was definitely Granny!

The other monkeys quickly gathered around this unusual creature. They looked really perplexed and Terry wondered if they could identify the strange little monkey as one of their own species. As for Granny, she had not seen her own kind for so long that being subjected to the scrutiny of these hairy beings must have been quite an ordeal. She responded very passively, and the group, their curiosity finally satisfied, began to wander away. Terry was delighted to see Granny following them, albeit at a much slower pace and without the glorious leaps and bounds of her fellow monkeys.

He decided to keep old Granny. The zoo vet was called. Together they devised a special diet to compensate for the deficiencies in her previous food and in the hope that it might make her fur grow again.

As the months went by, Granny made little improvement. Winter came and Terry could not believe she would survive. Every day, when he fed the monkeys, he looked out specially for Granny, half expecting to find that she had died in the night. But no, she struggled on. She spent most of the time in the warmth of the centrally-heated winter quarters and could only sit and watch as the other monkeys played in the snow, shaking branches and covering each other with the fascinating white powder.

Early the following year, Terry noticed that Granny had developed a swelling in her stomach. The vet was called once again to examine her. The lump could have been caused by a number of things, but he felt that at her age and in her condition an exploratory operation would undoubtedly prove fatal. Therefore they decided to let nature take its course in the hope that, as sometimes happens, the mysterious swelling would disappear. As the weeks went by, the lump grew and Granny became increasingly unattractive and even less active. The vet was called again. Having made sure that Granny was in absolutely no pain, he still believed that it was better to leave the swelling alone.

One day in early summer, Terry went looking for Granny and saw her sitting in a different spot than usual and looking quite changed. On closer inspection, he discovered that the swelling had disappeared. A sudden squeaking noise caught his attention. Granny heard it, too, and immediately started off in the direction of the sound. She led the way to a young member of the group, who had on its back a tiny, perfectly-formed baby squirrel monkey. As Granny approached, it squealed louder, so she fussed over it and eventually offered it her breast which the baby greedily accepted.

Terry wondered how he could have been so short-sighted! The obvious reason for Granny's lump had not even crossed his mind. She looked so old and worn out that it had not occurred to either him or the vet that the lump in Granny's stomach could have been caused by anything so simple as a baby! However, as with everything that happened to Granny, the birth was not absolutely straightforward, but the intelligent little monkeys had worked out their own method of coping with the problems which faced her. At birth a baby squirrel monkey immediately clambers on to the mother's back or stomach, clinging tightly to her fur for protection. Of course, Granny did not have any fur, so the baby had nothing to hang on to.

A young female squirrel monkey had stepped in and carried the baby for Granny. The baby quickly learned to squeak every time it needed feeding, whereupon Granny would immediately respond and fuss and cuddle her offspring while it fed. The shared parenthood scheme worked perfectly and the baby grew into a strong and healthy adult. Eventually she, too, had young and so poor, old, hairless Granny became a real granny in the end.

Below: *Squirrel monkeys are popular pets as babies, but they invariably prove to be too much to handle when they reach maturity.*

Sweetheart
The Tipsy Tawny Eagle

MANOR HOUSE WILDLIFE AND
LEISURE PARK

W hen the six-month-old African tawny eagle arrived, one look at the beautiful young bird caused Jo Williams to exclaim, 'What a sweetheart!' And so the eagle was christened!

During the next six months, Sweetheart was introduced to the way of life at Manor House, where there is a wide cross-section of birds of prey, including falcons, hawks, kestrels, vultures, and many others. In the summer months, a selection of the birds gives falconry displays. The displays take place around the manor which stands in the heart of the park's grounds. On hot summer days visitors buy themselves a drink and sit on the beautiful lawns around the house watching these magnificent birds demonstrate their remarkable aerial skills. Sweetheart was going to take part in these exhibitions.

Sweetheart learned quickly and, at first, behaved perfectly. It surprised everyone just how readily she joined the other birds and took part joyfully in the daily displays. Then one sunny June afternoon, she went missing during the display! At first the keeper thought that she had rested in a nearby tree, until he noticed a commotion going on around a picnic table outside the house. So had lots of children, who were also running excitedly in the same direction. Worried in case the bird was frightened by all the noise, the keeper dashed to the scene—only to see a very happy Sweetheart contentedly sharing a pint of beer with one of the visitors!

He could not believe his eyes. Looking as if they had been drinking pals in the same pub for years, the enormous tawny eagle and her male companion were relaxing over a pint and watching the world go by! It is very unusual to see a bird of prey drinking at all—let alone drinking beer! The bird retains water from its food and only rarely takes a drink.

Totally bewildered by this strange behaviour, Clive Williams hoped that it was an isolated instance and that after her alcoholic adventure Sweetheart would resume her natural drinking habits. But no! A few days later, Sweetheart yet again made an excursion during the display to fly down on to one of the picnic tables and began merrily supping from a visitor's beer glass!

Eventually Sweetheart's extraordinary behaviour was brought to the attention of the TV programme 'That's Life'. A visitor to the park had written to the programme to suggest that the eagle qualified perfectly for their talented pet feature. Obviously a representative from the programme had to confirm the extraordinary stories of the boozy bird, and so Tony Chapman visited Manor House to meet Sweetheart. Clive had to explain that the eagle certainly had not been trained to drink beer and that he could not guarantee that she would perform instantaneously. Nevertheless, he bought two pints of beer and sat at one of the picnic tables with Tony while the birds put on their usual display.

It was like magic. As Sweetheart soared above them, she appeared to look down and take a note of the brimming glasses of ale. Then she alighted on their table and began to drink from Tony's glass. Clive could hardly believe it—a planned routine could not have been better played. Naturally, Tony was delighted and wanted to bring the camera crew down to Manor House to record the eagle's bizarre antics as soon as he possibly could.

Within days, the park was swarming with cameramen, sound men, electricians, and the many other such technicians who were needed to film Sweetheart for the programme. The presenter was Michael Groth, who suggested that they should not only film Sweetheart supping ale but put her through a consumer test as well. Sweetheart completed the first part of her 'starring' role perfectly. But who knew what would happen in the consumer test? With just a little trepidation, Michael placed identical glasses of lager, cider, beer and lemonade in front of Sweetheart. She walked casually along the row of glasses, and barely sniffed the substitute drinks. One look at the pint of beer and she knew instantly what she wanted.

Sweetheart's fame spread and visitors to the park often asked to meet the beer-drinking eagle. So, to prevent Sweetheart from becoming an alcoholic, Clive now shows visitors the 'That's Life' video. The eagle has starred with Anneka Rice on the programme 'Treasure Hunt' and has a scrap-book virtually filled with press clippings. But like the greatest of stars, the publicity has not gone to her head and she can still be seen every day at Manor House, mixing and flying with her old friends as usual.

Overleaf: *Sweetheart, the tawny eagle who enjoys relaxing in the sun with a pint of beer.*

HELEN BYRT

Jeremiah
A Terror of a Toddler

BRISTOL, CLIFTON AND WEST OF ENGLAND ZOOLOGICAL SOCIETY

I t is peculiar how people will only see what they expect to see.

For instance, among the crowds of visitors to Bristol Zoo, one would expect to see a great number of doting parents with excited toddlers in tow. And in most cases that's all people do see. Only the most observant notice that one of the youngsters in the crowd looks slightly different. Not that his behaviour would provide any indication that he was anything but a normal, healthy, and curious three-year-old. Swinging along on the arms of his patient adult guardians, climbing on the railings, investigating bins and always trying to get into areas where he is strictly forbidden, is fairly typical of someone of his age. So it is little wonder that so many visitors pass Jeremiah, the baby gorilla, without a second glance. But Jeremiah is a very special toddler. Indeed, all gorillas are special. They are one of the world's most endangered species.

Jeremiah, a Western Lowland gorilla, was born in March 1984 and was the fifteenth gorilla to be born at Bristol Zoo. His father, Daniel, made history in 1971 by being the first of the species to be reared successfully in captivity in the United Kingdom. Normally, female gorillas rear their own young but, sadly, Jeremiah became very ill when he was just four months old and had to receive specialised medical treatment. Consequently, when he was returned to Delilah, his mother, her milk had dried up and so the keepers had to take on the demanding role of foster-mother. Although it was absolutely necessary for the keepers to carry out this function, it was a job that could not be taken lightly. Jeremiah's mother would naturally have taught Jeremiah gorilla behaviour and it was essential that he learned the same behaviour patterns to ensure that he would integrate with the group when he was older. It was also very important, however, as he was being reared on his own, that he had plenty of contact with the keepers and did not feel alone and insecure. Other than totally imitating the behaviour of a female gorilla and risking the chance of being carried off in a strait-jacket, the keepers had very carefully to effect a compromise in order to retain their own human and Jeremiah's gorilla status. Hence the regular walks round the zoo.

Twice daily, Mike Colbourne, the overseer of the ape section, takes Jeremiah out to join the human toddlers. Although the aim is to provide him with stimulation and exercise, the latter does not appear to have much importance to Jeremiah. Of far more interest are the different forms of seating around the park. From the ornamental benches to the concrete hippos, which make interesting seating for children, each one merits special investigation. But undoubtedly the best of all is the gate attendant's swivel stool. Hours of blissful gorilla-type fun can be derived from this simple form of seating. If he were allowed, Jeremiah would sit there all day, swinging to and fro on the fascinating moving chair. Visitors to the zoo invariably fail to notice the gate attendant's unusual, hairy assistant. We are waiting for the day when one such visitor asks Jeremiah for 'one adult, two under-threes, and a guide book'. But there is no truth in the rumour that Bristol Zoo will give Jeremiah the job on a permanent basis if he gives the correct change!

Almost as alluring are the zoo's wheel-chairs, which are kept specially to help those visitors who would find a walk around the zoo too arduous to enable them fully to enjoy their visit. Jeremiah regularly cons his keepers and the visitors into accepting that he falls into this category, and it has become one of his greatest treats to be pushed regally around the zoo, acknowledging his adoring public! Jeremiah has also developed his own version of sliding down banisters—a favourite game with all children. He uses the vinyl-topped rails which surround many of the animal enclosures. Carefully balancing himself on his tummy, he travels at considerable speed by pulling himself along, using the rails below for propulsion.

He has, however, been a little slower in learning those little niceties of behaviour necessary to ensure his continuing popularity as a local celebrity. As it is, being such a special chap, he receives a great many invitations to attend glamorous events—but as yet, he has failed to secure a repeat invitation to any of them! Perhaps it was the time that the new Lord Mayor and Lady Mayoress came to the zoo that caused news of Jeremiah's somewhat unpredictable response to the pressure of grand occasions to reach the ears of local hostesses. After all, prising off the Lady Mayoress's gleaming court shoe in the middle of a supposedly dignified welcoming ceremony, and then spending the entire event curiously smelling the inside while pulling expressions of complete disgust at the odours he was encountering, did nothing to enhance his reputation as a suave operator. Then again, the flower show incident might have been a contributory factor. He had only been invited to take part in the photo-call with the immaculately-groomed lady judge of the local flower arranging competition. But Jeremiah solemnly contemplated the winning entry with a suitably erudite air, and then, as if completely satisfied that it was indeed worthy of its prize, unexpectedly shot a hairy arm towards the elaborate arrangement, grabbed one of the blooms and calmly ate it. Strangely, there are no more flower shows in his social diary. The demand suddenly and mysteriously dried up.

During the summer months, Jeremiah's outings are given more purpose when he becomes the star guest of Bristol Zoo's 'Animal Encounters'. These informal afternoon sessions are extremely popular with both keepers and visitors. The visitors love having the opportunity to gain an insight into the workings of the zoo, while the keepers thoroughly enjoy sharing their knowledge and love of animals with caring people. All sorts of animals are introduced to the visitors, including snakes, elephants, and tapirs, but there is no doubt that Jeremiah attracts the most attention—and doesn't he know it!

Gorillas have always drawn crowds, partly due to the folklore which surrounds them but mainly, one supposes, because of their amazing similarity to ourselves. The first living gorilla to be seen in Europe was Alfred, who arrived at Bristol Zoo in 1930 and is still remembered with great affection by older Bristolians.

It is extremely difficult to contemplate, but there is a distinct possibility that the toddlers who delight in Jeremiah today may be the last generation to see a living gorilla. Poaching and loss of their forest homes are taking their toll on gorillas, as on all wild animals, and their numbers are very low indeed. It has been a long time since zoos took gorillas from the wild, but those who are the great-grandfathers of babies like Jeremiah have greatly helped to conserve their species. Today there is a world-wide breeding programme in zoos, and through national and international co-operation animals are loaned to ensure successful breeding. The Zoo Federation works with the Anthropoid Ape Advisory Panel, and together they research ways to breed Britain's captive gorillas in order to create a 'reservoir' in case gorillas do become extinct in the wild.

Is all this effort and money worth while? Well, when Jeremiah has yet again grubbied a clean blouse, nibbled a newly-polished shoe and altogether undermined one's dignity, there is no question about it. Yes, it's undoubtedly worth it!

Overleaf: *Jeremiah, a very special toddler.*

An Elephant Called Jubilee

THE NORTH OF ENGLAND ZOOLOGICAL SOCIETY, CHESTER

T here he was, son of Nobby and Judy, waiting to greet the keepers on their early arrival at the Elephant House on 8 May 1977. He did not realise it, but he was about to become a very famous baby—the first elephant successfully to be bred in the United Kingdom. Already a few hours old, he was moving around full of confidence. No real preparations had been made because although the pregnancy was obvious, no date for the birth was known, and we had no previous experience to draw on. Elephant pregacy-testing was not freely available in the 1970s—probably because of the lack of pregnant elephants! A blood sample from Judy the week before Jubilee was born did go to the laboratory, but before we received the findings, we had a very positive result of our own!

The elephant house presented a number of hazards to a new-born elephant. The island was surrounded by a dry moat; there was a deep bath; and with the two cows, there was a big African bull elephant. We decided that the first consideration should be the moat. With great speed a trailer-load of bales was spread around the bottom to cushion the fall should the baby topple in. It became obvious during this operation that the bull elephant was not going to be a problem. He was even more gentle towards the newcomer than the cows. So our next priority was the bath—seven metres square and two metres deep.

Many suggestions were made.

'Fill it with sand.'

'Not likely,' said the Clerk of Works, 'You'll fill up all my drains.'

'Fill it with bales of straw.'

'Not likely,' said the elephant keeper, 'The elephants will play football with them.'

Eventually, water became the obvious choice, although some worry was expressed as to whether Jubilee would drown if he fell in. And fall in he did—almost as soon as we had filled the bath right up. After what seemed an interminable length of time, he popped to the surface like a cork and was unceremoniously hooked out by mother Judy. After circling the island a couple of times, in he went again—and was fished out by Mum once more. This display of motherly care eased our minds, although we never saw him fall in again.

On the morning of Jubilee's birth, the zoo's founder and director, George Mottershead, was going away for a conference which was due to last a week. One of his life's ambitions had been to breed an elephant in Chester Zoo, and he delayed his departure to see the fulfilment of that ambition. Then, as he left, his last instruction to staff was, 'Make sure he's still here when I get back—or you won't be!' I think he probably meant it.

As Jubilee thrived, so did the zoo. It was one of the rare occasions when the North of England received national TV coverage for an animal story. Press photographers came by the dozen. Cameras arrived from 'Blue Peter', complete with John Noakes, and the programme's young viewers sent in thousands of suggestions for a 'name the new baby' competition. As it was Jubilee year, I suppose it was obvious what the most popular choice would be. At the time, we would have preferred a more appropriate name for an elephant, but that was the winner so we were stuck with it. Now, of course, we would find it strange to call him anything else.

An increase in the gate of a hundred thousand visitors was entirely due to the popularity of Jubilee, and the name quickly became associated with the animal. There are not many zoo animals who have become famous by their names. The only other ones that come to mind are Chi Chi the panda, Brumas the polar bear, and Guy the gorilla. Jubilee certainly fits into this category, and is probably the North's favourite animal. He is, too, the only one asked for by name in the zoo.

Jubilee's first birthday was quite an event. A local bakery produced a large cake, specially made with wholemeal bread; both local TV stations came and so did the usual battery of press photographers. The way that British animal lovers show their affection never ceases to amaze me. Jubilee receives letters, cards, and presents every Christmas and birthday. Some people even send him postcards when they are on holiday. Hundreds of cards arrived on his first birthday, but the peak was reached on his third. He received a staggering 3,840 birthday cards, many enclosing a cheque or postal order with the instruction, 'Please buy something special for a treat.' Jubilee was joined for those birthday celebrations by Stuart Hall, from the BBC's 'Northwest Tonight' programme. This time, Stuart came prepared, in his jogging gear. On a previous visit, he had worn a new suit, and after a very close encounter with the elephants, it smelt so awful that he threw it away!

Jubilee was a healthy baby. Apart from minor scrapes, our vet hardly needed to see him in a professional capacity. Both female elephants shared in his upbringing. He found at an early stage that 'Auntie' Sheba was more tolerant than Mother Judy, and with her he could get away with most things. His mother was much stricter, and would chastise him if she thought he was being naughty. Even so, if he was in trouble, it was Mum he wanted. A small squeak from him was enough to bring her running.

Jubilee is now ten years old. From that small start in life, at thirty-two inches (81 cm) tall and weighing 210 lbs (95 kg), he now stands at over two metres tall and weighs an estimated three tonnes. He has supreme confidence and is getting to the stage where he will challenge authority. As the old saying goes, 'Boys will be boys', and Sheba has been allowing him to play the man with her. There is growing optimism that this practice has led to pregnancy. Jubilee's father was a similar age when Jubilee was born.

Past experience has shown that dry moats are not really the answer to restraining an adult bull elephant. As Jubilee has grown, we have had to adapt the elephant house and paddock. This has been done by using old railway lines to make fences, hopefully capable of holding in the biggest bull, but also giving him plenty of room to exercise, while the pool allows him a chance to bathe. Jubilee is now installed in the new area, and has taken to it very happily.

His fame is spreading. Two adult cow elephants, in transit from Denmark to Belfast, have made a temporary stop at Chester for a couple of years, and hopefully will continue their journey in a pregnant state. Other enquiries have already been made for his services. He is, after all, one of only three Asiatic bulls in British zoos. With all the anticipated co-operation of the country's other elephant collections, Jubilee looks like being an important as well as a popular representative of his breed in the United Kingdom.

ROGER EDWARDS

A Tale of Two Tigers

THE ZOOLOGICAL SOCIETY OF GLASGOW AND WEST OF SCOTLAND

'T o be or not to be.' That was the question being faced unwittingly by the two tigers who had been living happily in an English zoo. The zoo was to be closed down and so their future was in jeopardy. They had to be found a new home or they might not be at all!

The owners of the zoo had found new homes for most of the smaller animals, but two tigers presented a more serious problem. Being such large animals, tigers require very specialised housing and diets. They are also expensive to look after as well as needing highly-trained keepers.

In a desperate effort to persuade someone that the pair was a desirable couple worthy of rehousing, they decided to explain their plight on national television. The tigers behaved beautifully in front of the cameras, giving the public a sample of all the best tiger-type poses. The effect was incredible and the tigers received hundreds of cards wishing them luck from viewers all over the country. But after three days there was still no definite offer of a home. Then a strange message came through to the zoo.

The tigers had been offered a new home but in Glasgow Zoo which, to everyone's knowledge, had not the correct type of accommodation available.

Although extremely grateful for the offer, the zoo owners were troubled in case they had misunderstood the message or it was some kind of joke. However, a long-distance telephone call to Glasgow revealed a story so full of coincidence and luck that it seemed almost too good to be true! Apparently, while their dilemma was being so dramatically relayed to the nation on BBC News, an artist was working hard on a portrait of a highly distinguished Nigerian chief, Bola Abimbola of the house of Adimula, who is a jetting-setting man of considerable wealth and influence. His vast family is spread throughout the world and his network of friends is enormous.

During the sitting, the artist kept the television turned on to ensure that this extremely energetic and busy man would remain still and occupied for more than a few seconds at a time. As luck would have it, the Chief saw the news item and was profoundly affected by the dilemma of the tigers.

Bola Abimbola decided to buy the pair and donate them to a zoo—but which one? The painter, being a loyal Glaswegian, naturally suggested Glasgow Zoo. At first this seemed a simple solution. That is, until they phoned the zoo director. The offer was terribly enticing, but Glasgow Zoo simply did not have an enclosure suitable for tigers, nor did it have sufficient funds to build one. It seemed as though the Chief's rescue plans would collapse—but being a man not used to being thwarted, he would not accept no for an answer.

If he could provide Glasgow Zoo with the tigers he could also provide them with a new enclosure! The Chief had a great many business associates in the west of Scotland who, with a little gentle persuasion, could be encouraged to help him to save the animals. And so it proved. A spacious site was chosen beside a river overlooking a golf course and the path of a Roman road. The architect went to work on a unique design to revolutionise tiger enclosures. Business contacts donated fencing, paving, bricks, wiring, plumbing—in fact, all the materials and skills which were necessary to construct the new enclosure. It was a demonstration of human generosity worthy of being called 'Tiger Aid'.

When the work was completed, the tigers travelled north to take up residence in their new and palatial home in Scotland. It is a palace for tigers. There are three dens. The main one has large windows which provide a spectacular view across the golf course and over the beautiful zoo gardens. Next to this is a more secluded area which is extremely useful when either of them needs a little peace and quiet. And finally, there is a cubbing den, which was used for the birth of their two female cubs. All these lead out on to their fabulous garden, which is full of trees and logs. There is a high platform, too, where they can soak up the sun and which provides a good vantage point from which to check out the visitors. Perhaps best of all is their own private swimming-pool. Unlike other members of the cat family, tigers love to have a paddle, especially when it gets hot during the summer, and the pool has been a tremendous amenity for them both.

When the tigers had finally settled in their new home, the zoo director threw a house-warming party. Hundreds of people flocked round to see the tigers and their new home. Cameras clicked; limousines rolled up and most of Glasgow's prominent citizens made the journey. Guests of honour were, of course, Chief Bola and members of his family. The Lord Provost of Glasgow arrived, wearing his official gold chain of office, and when he officially inaugurated the 'Adimula Tiger Den' everyone—even the tigers—heaved a huge sigh of relief that through people's kindness the magnificent tigers had not only been saved but also provided with one of the finest homes in the country!

Below: *Ben, happily rehoused in the Adimula Tiger Den at Glasgow Zoo.*

ROD RAYMENT

The Loneliness of the Long-Distance Crane Keeper

STAGSDEN BIRD GARDENS

T here is nothing like an early success to encourage you to make a decision which, in the long term, can result in unimagined escapades.

I suppose that is how we became inextricably involved with cranes. Obviously, I am not referring to the mechanical kind, but to the beautiful, though troublesome, feathered variety. Peter Kamininski and I took over Stagsden Bird Gardens from the founder of the Gardens, Fred Johnstone, in 1975. In 1984, we successfully bred some European grey cranes which were the first of the species to be bred in the United Kingdom.

After a success like that—a triumph made even sweeter by the fact that the pair had been in other collections for many years without breeding—the beginning of a rash scheme to specialise in keeping and breeding cranes began to formulate. When, later that year, our East African crowned cranes also did the honours, there was no turning back! Stagsden became a centre for cranes.

At the time it seemed an irresistible plan. Cranes are such impressive birds, with such intriguing and individual habits. Take, for instance, their unison call. Each species has its own peculiar sound which will carry for miles. Learning which call belonged to which species was absolutely fascinating. Then there are the babies. Anything small is adorable, but these tiny creatures, covered in a gingery down, which are able to run helter-skelter around the place a matter of twenty-four hours after hatching, are absolutely entrancing. More importantly, the crane is becoming extremely rare in the wild. Of the fourteen different species, six are acknowledged to be rare or endangered. Hence our very serious interest in rearing captive stocks.

The first cranes to arrive at Stagsden were a pair of the delicate demoiselle cranes. Their name aptly describes this fragile-looking, beautiful bird. However, it did not take us long to discover that appearances can be deceptive. Cranes have a very decorative and energetic courtship display, which involves an elaborate dance requiring room to leap around and spread their wings. Therefore, cranes are always kept in large open enclosures rather than conventional aviaries. To prevent them from disappearing out of their enclosures for ever, they are either wing-clipped or surgically pinioned.

At first we used wing-clipping, which meant that every year, after moulting, the birds had to be caught and their wings clipped again. Following our demoiselles' first moult, we cautiously entered their pen carrying catching nets, in order to restrain the birds while we carefully clipped the necessary wing feathers. It actually did not seem that difficult to us, especially as these particular birds were usually very tame and used to our presence. But one look at our nets and the male took fright, leapt high into the air and, despite having only one or two primary feathers, somehow managed to fly over the eight-foot fence, across the bird garden and into a neighbouring field! Horror-stricken, we set off in hot pursuit but, each time we neared the wayward bird, he decided to take off again. Finally the crane settled in a deep ditch, and we were able to recapture it. Worn out, muddy, exasperated but triumphant, we returned home. Without a second's hesitation, I telephoned the vet and instructed him to pinion the birds immediately. No more long-distance, cross-country runs for me!

When the unpinioned East African crowned crane arrived at the bird gardens to be paired with a single male bird, it took the vet several days before he could respond to our desperate requests for his services. But the new female seemed quite settled, choosing to roost on the top of a small shed and to jump down to rejoin the male in the morning. She had actually been wing-clipped, and we thought that this was probably sufficient to discourage her from disappearing until the vet could pay us a visit. We were wrong!

One windy evening, she began to call with the characteristic honking that we have now learned to associate with trouble! Gracefully, she launched herself into the air and, despite clipped wings, flew effortlessly over our east garden and alighted on a hill approximately half a mile away. Once again, we set off, armed with nets and shod in wellies. She led us a similar merry chase, disappearing into the skies the moment we were anywhere near her. Darkness fell, as we stood desperately waving our empty nets in the air, and we had to give up the chase. Downheartedly we returned to the Bird Gardens, planning to renew the trail at daybreak. Just before light, we both heard a familiar honking resounding over the bird garden. She'd returned home! We could not believe our ears. We shot out of bed, dressed hurriedly, and went out to locate her. She was finally spotted by a passer-by, who could not understand why the big bird was sitting outside the perimeter fence and could not appear to find the gate! My wife successfully ushered the crane back into the gardens, where we eventually recaptured her. The pair of cranes finally settled down happily together and produced several clutches of eggs.

The work at Stagsden continues, despite some hilarious and strenuous incidents. We are breeding rare birds on a regular basis and, although not all the eggs prove fertile, we are hopeful that eventually we shall succeed in breeding all species, including the very rare white-naped crane.

Overleaf: *Of the fourteen different species of crane, six are acknowledged to be rare or endangered.*

George and his State Registered Rhino Nurse

KNOWSLEY SAFARI PARK

I t was November 1977, and it appeared likely that the birth of Knowsley Safari Park's first white rhino would coincide with that of Princess Anne's first child. As the births were both of considerable national importance, Mr Tennant, the General Manager of the park, thought it appropriate to honour the event by naming their new arrival after the royal baby. But, somehow, Peter the Rhino did not ring true.

So, with a little thought, another name was chosen, one which had been associated with the crown of Britain for many centuries —George! Unfortunately, George's start in life was nowhere near as auspicious as that of young Peter Phillips. Maggie, George's mother, took one look at her offspring and immediately kicked him out of her stable!

Mr Tennant and David Ross, the Curator, who had attended the important birth, were at hand to rescue the baby rhino. They sat up all night with the little animal, who was so hungry and dejected that he squealed for his mother continuously, but this appeared to have no effect upon her. In the morning they tried once again to introduce George to his mother. Her reaction was immediate and decisive. She simply threw him out of the stable again. Tennant recalls: 'There was absolutely no way that George would survive with his mother, therefore we were faced with the option of hand-rearing, which is never the best way.'

The immediate problem was giving the obviously ravenous youngster something to eat. The constitution of rhino milk is very similar to that of a pig and so a special mixture was concocted. 'Mother' was David, with a lemonade bottle full of this special brew, and an adapted lamb's feeding teat attached. Hungrily George sucked one bottle—then another—then another. Only after he had completely emptied five full bottles did he appear satisfied and ready to sleep. David, who became responsible for the feeds, thought that this enormous appetite might just be the result of having been so traumatically rejected by his mother and going without a feed for twelve hours—little did he know!

George's appetite did not diminish in the slightest. In fact, as the weeks went by, David began to feel that all he ever did with his time was to feed this voracious baby. Day and night were spent planning, preparing, and producing George's food. One bottle lasted only a matter of seconds.

During this period, George lived in a stable at the back of David's house in the centre of the wildlife park. During the day the young rhino played in the stable yard with David's basset-hound puppy. Sadly, at times George did not understand that he now weighed around ninety kilos, and he used to think that he could get up to the same antics as the dog. After all, if the basset could run in and out of the kitchen so could he—despite the fact there were a few obstacles in the way. After all, what is a glass-panelled door to a young rhino! In his eagerness to join his canine chum, George simply did not notice that the door was closed and barged straight through it! George did not suffer—but the door certainly did!

Normally, after about three months, a young rhino will begin to nibble at grass and gradually wean itself from its mother. Not so George. He enjoyed his milk and refused even to contemplate eating grass. By the time he was six months old, he was drinking his feed from a huge, shallow tub and at the height of his milk consumption, he was devouring 112 litres of pig milk a day.

George's refusal to eat dry food had serious implications and caused his health to deteriorate. Although David bulked up the milk by dissolving into it special feeding nuts containing extra vitamins and minerals, so forming a porridge-like mixture, George suffered constantly from stomach and skin disorders, which are the first and most obvious indications of an inadequate diet. As George had no real mother to imitate and learn from he had to be persuaded to sample dry food, which required a great deal of time and patience. And so a surrogate mother was hired in the form of a qualified State Registered Nurse, who was able to spend all day with George.

Pam, the nurse, would take George on long walks around the safe areas of the park and sit with him, gently putting hand-pulled grass into his mouth in the hope that he might just find it tasty and so be encouraged to investigate the green stuff around him for himself. But George would have none of it and every time grass was put between his lips he spat it out. This went on throughout the summer—much to the bemusement of the visiting public, who naturally found the sight of a young woman leading round a white rhino and stuffing grass into his mouth somewhat perplexing!

Despite Pam's devoted attention George occasionally managed to slip away, usually with disastrous results. One day, he decided to investigate the camels more closely. As it turned out, the camels objected to such close scrutiny from such a young and obviously ill-mannered rhino and expressed their displeasure by biting his ear!

As the weather grew colder, it became obvious that George was not going to change his diet and David had nothing to look forward to but a long, cold winter of preparing rhino gruel. It turned out to be a tortuous winter, with George being constantly ill and in need of close supervision. David and Mr Tennant longed for him to understand that the hay, carrots, nuts, and other dry stuffs that they continually tried to persuade him to swallow, would cure all his ills.

The spring brought the new season's sweet-smelling grass, and so David, rather half-heartedly, took George out, in the forlorn hope that he might just get the idea and begin to graze. George lowered his head to the ground. He sniffed, and looked quizzically at David. Then down went his head again, and he began chewing the grass in enormous gulps. As if by magic, George had finally got the right idea. David felt as though massive weights had been lifted from his shoulders. No more tubs of food—no more endless treks to and from George's stable and, most important, no more ill health!

From that precise moment, George began to improve. He went from strength to strength and has now grown to be a larger-than-average, adult male rhino. His size is particularly pleasing as it is generally considered that hand-reared animals do not develop as well as those naturally reared.

Below: *White rhino George drains another bottle of David Ross's special brew!*

GRAHAM CATLOW

Camel Carnival

BLACKPOOL MUNICIPAL ZOOLOGICAL GARDENS

W hen the invitation to take part in a carnival procession along Blackpool's promenade arrived, it appeared too tempting an offer to refuse. Mind you, this was in the formative years of Blackpool Zoo, when the staff were all younger and more adventurous, and so more prepared to enter into such escapades.

There were three likely candidates for the adventure: a trained camel known as Achmed, McGinty the goat, and a partially-trained llama called Philippa. Since the keepers could not choose between them, it was decided to take all three. After all, if Blackpool Zoo was going to be represented in this prestigious parade, it might as well put on a good performance! The procession was exactly a month away, during which the animals had to be trained and fully prepared to face the unusual sights of the exotic carnival floats which participate annually in the parade. Achmed presented a further problem for the keepers: at that time, the zoo did not own a vehicle large enough to transport camels. If Achmed was to take part—and he would undoubtedly be the show-stopper of the parade— the difficulty of covering the journey from Blackpool Zoo to the starting point for the parade had to be resolved.

The keepers estimated that it was about four miles to the start; but walking there and back, having followed the entire processional route, would involve a journey of a little over ten miles! Although camels are naturally adapted to walking long distances, Achmed had grown used to the soft life. The extent of his normal exercise was a leisurely stroll around the grounds, stopping to talk to the visitors, and generally taking his own time. If he was to be fit enough to take part, Achmed had to go into immediate training—so had the keepers who were to accompany him!

The idea of taking Achmed out on to the roads around Blackpool appealed to his keepers. The daily excursion offered a real change from their daily routine and was an opportunity of which to take advantage, despite reservations about the problems that the camel's potentially dangerous reactions to traffic, shops, noise, and excitement could present. Each day the route was extended and

Right: *Achmed, the show-stopping camel at Blackpool's carnival procession.*

revised to ensure that Achmed faced every possible contingency. The keepers' ingenuity in planning these trips knew no bounds! The local hospital became a regular port of call and Achmed, having stretched his legs, was allowed to graze the grass outside the children's ward, or sometimes the nurses' quarters! The visiting camel delighted both the staff and the patients, and perhaps helped the younger ones forget their troubles for short while, for the nurses would carry the more sickly children to the window, to ensure that Achmed's company was appreciated by all.

His fame as a lawn-mower grew, and he was in great demand, particularly in certain keepers' gardens. While Achmed did the job of their machines, his handlers helped themselves to their own versions of light refreshment. The route that was most favoured allowed the ship of the desert to have a temporary berth. He was tied up alongside the multi-coloured modern transportation in a hostelry car park. Here he was able to quench the thirst that walking round the lanes of the Fylde had given him. The landlord, however, never seemed completely at ease when he took the order for 'three pints, please — and one for the camel'!

The day of the procession arrived. It was a true carnival day —wet and windy. Achmed and his zoo keepers rose early. The walk had been carefully timed to the last minute. Nothing had been left to chance—well, almost nothing! That is one of the problems of working with animals. One can never be absolutely sure what they will do, however much time, effort, and work has been spent trying to anticipate everything. It was arranged that the keepers bringing Philippa the llama and McGinty the goat in the zoo van would arrive more or less simultaneously with Achmed, their estimated time of departure having been carefully calculated to ensure this.

Everything began splendidly. Achmed performed beautifully, and his keepers, despite the early hour, were bright and eager. They walked happily, as planned, to the congregation point of the procession and, despite the rain, arrived in good time, ready to join the fun of the carnival. But—where was everybody else? There was no sign of the zoo van, and most of the other people taking part in the parade seemed to have disappeared. The party from Blackpool Zoo stood forlorn, bedraggled, and somewhat mystified. They could not have made a mistake about the starting time, as the instruction papers had been read and re-read and they had definitely come to the right place, as the abandoned carnival floats proved.

Eventually, an official told them that the procession had been delayed for two hours in the hope that the weather would improve. The zoo had been contacted about the changes in plan, but unfortunately Achmed and the keepers had already begun their arduous journey!

The delay was not long enough to allow them to return to the zoo, nor sufficiently brief to be shrugged off as a temporary hitch. All they could do was doggedly to face the fact that the two hours facing them would be wet, uncomfortable, and largely unbearable! At last, however, the weather cleared, and the zoo van arrived with the other animals and their keepers. McGinty took the lead, Philippa followed, and Achmed brought up the rear. The zoo van drove in front to help advertise the delegation, and all looked set for an enjoyable event, in spite of the inauspicious start.

But as the band struck up, Philippa sat down!

She had been carefully coached, and had been prepared for all sorts of unusual sights, but no one had foreseen the problems that a brass band might cause. At the opening chord, the reluctant llama, as if on command, sat and refused to budge! Coaxing, bribery, coercion—nothing would shift her. The parade had begun and as the gap between the animals and the float in front widened, the people behind began to mutter impatiently and to offer 'helpful' suggestions as to how to move Philippa. The only solution was to reverse the zoo van and bodily manhandle her into it. So, much heaving and straining later, with the llama safely enclosed in the van, and with Blackpool Zoo's representation depleted by one, the procession restarted.

As the company walked, the sun gradually came out, turning the once wet, miserable conditions warm and humid. The procession wound its way round the streets of Blackpool. Achmed began to relax and thoroughly to enjoy himself. He slowed down and stopped pulling, walking with a steady plod, which suited his keepers admirably. He remained at this pace to the end of the procession, where McGinty joined Philippa in the van, to be transported in comparative luxury back to the zoo.

Achmed and the keepers began the trek home, by now a daunting proposition. As they neared the zoo, Achmed, being no fool, recognised the familiar territory. Visions of his dry stable, food, warmth, comfort, and camel-type luxuries ran through Achmed's mind. Off he set at a pace hitherto unknown in zoo camels. As they were dragged along behind, the footsore and weary keepers were almost at breaking point. It was the last straw! From that day no one dared even whisper camel and carnival in the same breath for fear of instant reprisal.

DAVE BROWN

Merlin the Mynah, and Other Precious Species

PADSTOW TROPICAL BIRD GARDENS

D ave Brown and his wife, Pat, have recently taken over Padstow Tropical Bird Gardens in North Cornwall from Dave's father, Jack, who in 1968 cleared several acres of hillside overlooking Padstow and the Camel estuary to build a centre to further his passion for tropical birds, and especially for endangered species. By 1970, the site was ready to open to the public and since then its reputation has soared.

Visitors are impressed by the immaculately-kept gardens, where the flora and fauna are an attraction in their own right, and by the carefully organised flights which are individually designed to suit the particular needs of the inhabitants, and offer pretty much five-star accommodation.

Richard and Simon, the gardens' keepers, are crucial to life at the Tropical Bird Gardens, where the breeding and rearing of endangered species, especially soft-billed birds, is pushing the zoo to the forefront of world achievement. They are devoted to the birds in their care and they feed babies —any babies—at two-hourly intervals through the day *and night*, after first carefully preparing the food.

It is this systematic care and attention to detail that has enabled the Padstow Tropical Bird Gardens successfully to breed a number of species for the first time in the United Kingdom, and Dave Brown is justifiably proud that in the summer of 1987 his team was able to hand-rear a crimson toucanet from a few days old, when its mother died—a world first.

To the staff, every bird and many of the butterflies (they are bred there, too) has its own personality, but there are a few who inevitably stand out in the crowd and for the crowds. Of the impressive macaws, Mac (blue-and-gold) and Charlie (green-winged) are pretty selective about their behaviour. Mac will only perform his many little tricks if he feels the audience is large enough and appreciative enough. Charlie is very fussy and will only allow the keepers to handle him if they are wearing a particular type of blue anorak. Merlin the mynah bird, at the far end of the gardens, is a major attraction with his extensive vocabulary, but he does have a peculiar aversion to microphones. Try to record his hilarious comments and he becomes as secretive and silent as the Mafia. Even the most prim of people would approve of the lilacine Amazon parrots who live a very proper life. They will only mate when the lights are out and they are sure no one is looking. In the public eye, they show no affection towards each other at all.

One of the outstanding features at Padstow is the tropical house itself, where visitors may mingle with the birds in conditions of jungle humidity. But keep your eye on the passion flower, because then you may have a chance of spotting the Hardwickes fruitsucker before he spots you and launches himself at you in a fearless and fearsome 'dive-bomb' raid! Very brave, for such a small and delicate bird.

Below: *The Tropical Bird Gardens at Padstow are at the forefront of world achievement in breeding rare and endangered species of birds, such as blue and gold macaws.*

Morning Inspection

SOUTHPORT ZOO

I t takes Doug Petrie an age to complete the morning inspection of his zoo in Southport. Not that it is a particularly large zoo—in fact it would not be unfair to describe Southport as being one of the smaller zoos in the Federation. Neither has he to feed or clean the animals, as that work is carried out by his keepers. His tour begins at six a.m., long before the people who come to the zoo have even contemplated rising. The first port of call is to his beloved binturongs which are perhaps his favourite animals. It is little wonder that these hairy, bear-like animals, which look something like a cross between a raccoon and over-sized tom-cat, are so near to his heart. They are gentle, friendly creatures whose clown-like antics when playing together never fail to amuse. Doug's group of binturongs is the most successful in the United Kingdom, to which almost every example of the species in British Zoos is related. In all he has successfully bred twenty-four binturongs, and the latest youngsters are now being reared by their natural mothers. Twelve of them still live together at Southport. There's Buster, Bertha, Blossom, Becky, Bellulah, Booboo and Betsy, in addition to five others who are awaiting christening. Trouble is, Doug is running out of names beginning with B. Suggestions are welcome! Becky and Booboo, which Doug personally hand-reared, are particularly attached to him.

Leaving the fascinating binturongs is difficult for Doug, but a few yards further on are the garrulous cockatoos, Cocky and Henrietta, who, incidentally, arrived at Southport a Henry but was soon discovered to be a female and quickly renamed. Immediately the birds spot him they squawk, 'Hello . . . come over here . . . Hello . . . come over here.' Anxiously, they climb up the front of their enclosures and lift their wings or put their heads on one side, waiting for Doug gently to stroke their feathers. Attempts to continue his tour are thwarted when the birds begin their usual chorus of protests: 'Come back here . . . come back here!'

Cindy and Candy greet him next. Purring like two domestic pussy cats, the two full-grown lionesses run to meet him and wait for Doug to stroke them. Both mother and daughter spent their cubhood in the Petrie household and are consequently great friends with Doug's Alsatians, too. Dogs, man and big cats unite in a friendly early morning welcome. Doug imitates the lionesses' greeting noises and lets them know that he is just as pleased to see them looking bright and well as they are to see him.

All the characters from Pets Corner, an area of the zoo which resembles a small farmyard, demand their fair share of attention, too. The old ponies whose working lives are over and who now spend their days lazily munching hay and carrots, the ram who cannot stand the company of other sheep, the donkeys and the deer, all greet Doug like a long-lost friend.

Bubbles and Fu, the small-clawed oriental otters, are a little more reticent than the other animals. They peer at Doug from the entrance to their den, but wait to be cajoled and coaxed before deigning to talk. Squeaking and chattering excitedly, the pair of otters then tease Doug by bobbing in and out of their den, preventing him from getting a clear view of them.

Looking at the magnificent mandrills, Doug finds it hard not to recall Bella, the first mandrill to be bred at Southport and the first to be bred in Britain for twenty years. She had to be hand-reared, but grew to produce and rear many youngsters of her own. Indeed, the eight females currently at Southport are all related to Bella. Of course, there have been different fathers. When the original male died, Doug was given another by London Zoo, called Fritz, and before Fritz died he produced one son which Doug was able to exchange with Dudley Zoo for an unrelated male, Jasper, and so continue the breeding programme of what had then become an endangered species.

Jasper was then seventeen and had not produced any offspring in spite of continual efforts to persuade him to do so. Doug is always very careful when introducing a new animal into an established group but, much to his amazement, within five days, two of the females showed a great deal of interest in this handsome new male in their midst. Within the year, Jasper became a father for the first time and has continued to sire mandrills successfully ever since.

Having spent time with the many different species of monkey, with the penguins, leopards and others, Doug finally finds himself in front of the gibbon enclosure, where the family group which lives there has bred very successfully, despite having arrived at Southport with a record of being non-breeders.

When Doug has finished his tour and is reassured that all his animals are fit and well, the zoo opens to the public. In the evening he will repeat the exercise, although this time he will softly call all the animals by name and they will retire for the night into their evening enclosures. Southport is a particularly friendly place and remarkable in the way that all the animals respond to the voice of Doug Petrie —except, of course, the fish, but he is working on that!

ANDREW HAYWORTH-BOOTH

The New Arrivals

WINDSOR SAFARI PARK

T he park was completely overrun by newsmen, some accompanied by film crews, others swathed in expensive Nikon cameras; definitely not the most normal of days at Windsor Safari Park!

The focus of all the media activity was a killer whale who was about to take his place in Seaworld as a mate for Winnie, the resident female. Such a delicate operation required much planning and highly detailed organisation. Lifting the enormous marine mammal, who weighed around seven tonnes, out of the transporter and lowering him gently into his new pool was a highly complex and skilled task requiring the constant supervision of the zoo vet, the management and keepers.

Half way through the operation, one of the journalists wandered away from the main press group and peered into the nursery pool at the rear of the public area. On her return she enquired about the age of the baby dolphin she had just been watching. The keeper, rather impatient that his concentration had been disrupted, replied hastily, 'That's Juno. He's just one year old.'

'I had no idea that young dolphins were so small,' the journalist replied.

It took a split second for the implication of her casual comment to hit home. The keeper left his post and raced round to check whether what he suspected could be true. In the pool where, only half an hour before, there had been three dolphins, there were now four! Honey, the expectant mum, had given birth—and she had chosen the worst possible moment to do so!

The keeper immediately went to find Dave Lindsay, Seaworld's senior keeper, to tell him the exciting news. Dave could hardly believe it—of all the days to choose! He knew that Honey was due to give birth, of course, but it was almost as if she knew that the press would be around in force and so she would be able to create the same kind of media excitement that had greeted the birth of Juno the year before. Juno was the first dolphin to be born and successfully reared by his mother in Great Britain and so was of enormous interest to the public and press alike.

It had been in January 1984 when Dave first noticed that Lulu, Juno's mother, had started to put on a lot of weight round her middle. She had been swimming with Smarty, the male, and it seemed very likely that Windsor Safari Park could have a pregnant female on its hands. Every day, the dolphins and killer whales perform a series of exercises. These have far more than a purely entertainment value. As well as keeping them fit, they help to keep the minds of these highly intelligent animals alert. During these sessions, the dolphin keepers can never be sure exactly what the dolphins are going to do and are continually surprised at the tricks they pull. Lulu was one of the worst for teasing. Being the clown of the group, she loved to pretend that she did not understand a word Dave said, and then, as soon as his back was turned in total exasperation, she would carry out the exercise to perfection—even adding her own elaboration at times! But the obvious increase in girth meant that her daily routines had to be modified and her diet adapted to suit an expectant mum.

Below: *The dolphins at Windsor Safari Park's Seaworld have been entertaining audiences for years with their comical antics and routines, while also being part of an important breeding programme for the zoo.*

At first Lulu was not asked to take part in the daily performances, but when Dave noticed that she was doing the exercises all by herself and was obviously missing the activities, he devised a programme especially for her, which eliminated particularly muscular feats such as aerial spins. These dolphin ante-natal exercises ensured that Lulu was happy and fit during her pregnancy. On 8 June, Dave had noticed that she was far less active than usual. By his calculations, he knew that she must be almost ready to give birth, and her behaviour certainly suggested that this was the case. He transferred Lulu into a back pool where he could control the number of visitors. He also put Angie, another dolphin, into the same pool to act as a companion and 'Auntie'. Being highly gregarious mammals, total isolation could have proved very stressful.

The staff at Windsor worked in rotas to keep an eye on Lulu, checking her every movement and watching for any tell-tale signs that the birth was beginning. Then at nine p.m. they observed about five centimetres of the baby's tail fluke—the birth had started.

It takes about an hour for a dolphin to give birth. While they waited anxiously, night fell, and they lost sight of the mother completely. They had torches, but decided that it was best to let the birth occur as naturally as possible. All of a sudden, in the pitch black, silent evening, they heard a surge of splashing and whistling and the deep breathing of Lulu was accompanied by the soft blowing of her baby! She'd done it . . . all on her own!

The keepers anxiously shone their torches around the surface of the pool and suddenly before them was a tiny, perfect replica of Lulu, coming up for air and then swimming confidently beside its mother! A round of cheers broke the tense silence, as the Windsor staff celebrated the momentous occasion.

The birth of Neptune, exactly one year after Juno, was an equally dramatic occasion—if only because of Honey's impeccable timing! When Honey looked near to giving birth she was put into the same pool as Juno and Lulu, and half-hourly progress checks were made. However, a particularly short birth had enabled Honey to produce Neptune between checks. Fortunately, Neptune proved a healthy and strong baby.

When the calves met each other, they got on immediately and Neptune has obviously learned a lot from his older step-brother. He developed far more quickly and reached particular stages weeks before Juno had. This could also be a reflection of the different nature of their mothers, as Honey was far less protective, leaving young Neptune alone to explore far earlier than Lulu. The 'boys' are great rivals and are constantly jostling each other for attention. It is very difficult not to draw parallels with boys of the same age, as they have mock battles and pop their heads cheekily out of the water to check if Dave is still watching them. They undoubtedly look as if they are smiling and appear to have a tremendous sense of humour. Watching the two youngsters at play, it is so very easy to understand why the dolphin evokes so many romantic and mystical images.

FIONA PRINGLE

Penguins on Parade

THE ROYAL ZOOLOGICAL SOCIETY OF SCOTLAND, EDINBURGH

I t is often said that the two most interesting landmarks in Scotland's capital city are the Castle and the penguin parade at Edinburgh Zoo. It is therefore hardly surprising that around two-thirty p.m., the atmosphere at the famous penguin enclosure is electric. Visitors have gathered from all parts of the grounds, eagerly jostling one another in order to ensure that they get a good view. Youngsters are gently pushed to the front, weaving their way between adults' legs, while others are hoisted up on parental shoulders above the heads of the waiting crowds.

The appearance of two keepers hushes the crowd, who willingly respond to the keepers' efforts to cleave a straight, uninterrupted line through the confusion. The anticipation mounts and youngsters, too impatient to keep still any longer, suddenly rush to the front, desperate not to miss a single moment of what will be the highlight of their visit to the zoo. Suddenly, the gates open and out march the penguins to a blaze of flash-bulbs, a crescendo of clicking camera shutters, and squeals of delight from onlookers of all ages. Edinburgh Zoo's famous penguin parade has begun.

The parade has become a tradition at the zoo. It all began in about 1946, when a less-than-alert keeper accidentally left open the gates to the penguin enclosure. The birds calmly followed the keeper out of their enclosure and stood behind him. At first he did not realise what had happened, but when he looked over his shoulder, he was absolutely amazed to discover that he was being followed by a group of inquisitive penguins!

The unexpected parade created considerable interest with the media and visitors alike, and the keeper was asked to repeat the performance so many times that the zoo decided to devise a regular penguin parade every day during the summer season.

One of the most experienced participants in today's parades is a magnificent penguin known as Toni Poe, who is the oldest king penguin in the collection and still takes part in the daily outing.

As soon as the gate to their enclosure is opened, Toni Poe and the rest of the king penguins attempt to lead the way out—their efforts being constantly thwarted by the inquisitive gentoo penguins. As there are well over ninety gentoos and only twenty-seven kings, the smaller birds somehow always manage to be at the front, busybodying their way through the crowds. The king penguins, as their name suggests, have a regal air, and like to walk together with a certain dignity. The gentoos, however, have no such ideas about status and appearance.

The visitors who line the route have to hold tightly on to their belongings, as nothing escapes the curious beaks of the gentoos. They see nothing wrong in rummaging through a complete stranger's picnic hamper before proceeding on their journey.

Worst of all, if the keepers who lead the procession do not keep a very keen eye open for all the gentoos, one of the more adventurous is bound to feel the urge to explore the zoo grounds. The trouble is, they get so far and then suddenly realise that they do not know the way back, and panic! A few yards can seem like a few thousand miles to a small penguin.

Keeping the birds 'on parade' becomes easier during March and April, when the gentoos become far too interested in the process of breeding to steal the limelight from the king penguins. And what a palaver they make about it!

First of all, they have to instruct their keepers exactly where to put their nesting rings. These have to be inch perfect in exactly the same spot as they were the previous nesting season. The only way the gentoos can direct this activity is by pecking the keepers' ankles until each bird is entirely satisfied with the positioning of its ring. So, around 15 March, many of Edinburgh's penguin keepers develop a certain hobble as a direct result of the birds' constant attacks on their ankle bones!

It does not stop there! Next, there is the ceremony of the stone selection! To the average eye, a pebble is a pebble is a pebble—but that is certainly not the case to the discerning eyes of the broody female gentoo. The male has to present her with nicely rounded stones which measure 2.5 cm in diameter. And even if he manages to fill her nest with stones all of that exact dimension, she is more than likely to take a fancy to the pebbles in her neighbour's nest and send her poor mate off on a foraging mission. And all this in the name of love!

The king penguins, as ever, treat the process of courtship with far greater dignity. They do not disrupt the whole colony with their demands. Around July, the males enthusiastically serenade their females, and they lovingly preen each other. Each female then lays one egg, which it keeps on its feet, protected by a flap of skin. This enables the birds to walk around, but, naturally enough, during this time they do not take part in the penguin parade.

As Edinburgh has the largest colony of king penguins in Britain, and is able to breed them regularly, the birds are in tremendous demand from the media. Indeed, the company which produces the famous chocolate biscuits of the same name has filmed the birds for its television commercials. Recently, a programme was made about the Edinburgh Festival Fringe and the presenter decided that he had to interview one of the penguins, as they were so representative of the town. Patiently, he placed himself in the centre of the parade, without being absolutely sure what would happen. The birds did not need any rehearsal. Toni Poe simply stole the whole scene. She calmly walked over and obligingly nodded and shook her head on cue when interviewed. It was, perhaps, all part of the king penguins' plan to ensure that they never become overshadowed by the interfering gentoos—although it would be hard to imagine that, despite their hilarious antics, any birds could steal the scene from the magnificent kings.

Below: *P–P–P–P–Penguins on p–p–p–parade at Edinburgh zoo.*

MARTIN GOYMOUR

There's no Leopards like Snow Leopards

BANHAM ZOO

'Snow leopards were the perfect solution to our problem,' explained Martin Goymour, the proprietor of Banham Zoo in Norfolk. 'We had specialised in breeding rare and endangered species of primates, especially tamarins and marmosets, and had earned a considerable reputation world-wide for our successes. However, the results of visitor questionnaires told us that they would also appreciate seeing some larger animals, especially big cats.

'The policy of Banham has always been to concentrate entirely upon those species which could very soon become extinct in the wild, and so we had to think very carefully about how we could continue to live up to our ideals, as well as satisfy the public. After all, without the support of our visitors, both in terms of admission charges and sponsorship, we would not be able to continue our work. An ideal solution presented itself when Helsinki Zoo told us that they had a female snow leopard who desperately needed an unrelated mate. Having established a close relationship with Helsinki Zoo through our work with marmosets, we were able to discuss the possibility of exchanging animals—as long as we could find a suitable young male snow leopard.

'Snow leopards are one of the world's most threatened species. There are only an estimated four hundred left in the wild, and these are continually subject to the greed of hunters. Theirs is perhaps the finest coat of all cats. The unusual cream and black colour, and its extra thickness caused by the cold climates of Nepal and Tibet from which it originates, makes the snow leopard's pelt highly desirable amongst those who wear fur coats —despite the obvious fact that it looks much better on the snow leopard than it ever could on a human's back!' Martin added, sadly.

'Whilst Bulgan [the female snow leopard] was all alone in Scandinavia, I discovered that across the Atlantic in Milwaukee there was a young and solitary male who would benefit from such a beautiful mate.'

So all arrangements were finalised. Martin worked with the zoos and the appropriate authorities to ensure that the two cats would arrive in their new East Anglian home at about the same time, so that they could spend the statutory quarantine period of six months together to enable them to get accustomed to one another. Yamdi, the brash young American, arrived on schedule and duly waited in the quarantine quarters for the imminent arrival of Bulgan. The poor young male waited and waited—and it wasn't until his quarantine period was almost over that the blushing bride deigned to make her appearance—five months late!

'I decided that we would have to stick to our original scheme, and so extend Yamdi's period of isolation with Bulgan alongside to keep him company. With such precious animals it was essential to do all we could to ensure that they would get along together and prevent any chance of them fighting. When the great day came for them to be let out into their outdoor enclosure it was quite an occasion. I had images of them running round the new-found space together, rather like those romantic slow-motion scenes from commercials when young lovers frolic through the countryside! But nothing could have been further from the truth. They completely and utterly ignored each other! Each behaved as if there had been only one snow leopard in the enclosure—and that was him or her! Talk about giving one another the cold shoulder; they should have been called ice leopards!

'Things didn't improve much when we moved them into their brand new enclosure. Whilst in quarantine I had been supervising the final touches to a new leopard house, which was to be their permanent home. Prior to moving day, we spent a great deal of time rehearsing the procedure. Beautiful as they are, snow leopards are highly dangerous animals and so we had to make sure that we could cope with any emergencies should there be the slightest hitch. Dry runs with capture equipment, and routines in the case of an escape, were practised with great attention paid to every detail. As it was, everything went according to plan.

'The new enclosure had the effect we hoped it would, and Yamdi and Bulgan became inseparable. So much so, that exactly one year to the day that they were moved, they produced two fabulous cubs! The birth of the snow leopard cubs is perhaps our greatest achievement to date. The cubs are so adorable, the next problem will be having to part with them in the future! Somehow I don't think it will be at all surprising if a new leopard enclosure appears at Banham in the near future, especially designed for the two young snow leopard cubs!'

Overleaf: *Snow leopards are one of the world's most threatened species. There are only an estimated four hundred left in the wild.*

PAMELA JOHNSTONE

A Life Full of Otters

MOLE HALL WILDLIFE PARK

I t was 25 December, and the family was eagerly waiting to tuck into the traditional Christmas fare—turkey, plum pudding, brandy butter, and all the usual glorious festive food. We had taken our places round the table, mouths watering and tummies rumbling, when all of a sudden we all heard loud scratching noises at the front door.

I had to go and investigate—hard as it was to leave my plate, which was by this time brimming with food. Somewhat grudgingly, I opened the front door, and looked out. There was no one to be seen—until I lowered my gaze and saw four otters tumble through the door and land at my feet! They were obviously filled with Christmas spirit, and were filling the air with excited otter noises. However, much as they would have enjoyed the turkey, I could not allow them to run riot through the house!

Our otters loved eels, and if anything could work to lure them back to their enclosure, it would be the temptation of a luscious eel. Waggling one eel behind me, I managed successfully to lure the otters back to their enclosure. Hard as we looked, we could not discover how they had managed to escape. Proper little Houdinis, we thought!

Eventually we gave up the search and returned to our rapidly-cooling Christmas feast. We then settled down to celebrate, as families do, with Christmas crackers, candles, mottos and silly hats. All seemed at peace in the world—for about half an hour! Then an ominous 'scratch, scratch' at the front door suggested that the persistent otters had returned. I could not believe my ears!

There they were again, on the doorstep, waiting to come in. Thankfully, the eel trick worked again. So, back we all went to their enclosure, with me in the lead, rather like the Pied Piper of Hamelin. It was only then that I noticed that the level of the water in their sunken pool was incredibly high. Someone had left the tap on, so it was quite easy—when the water level rose, the otters simply swam out!

In spite of that Yuletide aggravation, the otters at Mole Hall are our pride and joy. They are such individual characters, and all of them, both past and present, are indelibly imprinted on our memories. There have been otters at Mole Hall since 1960 and, in the early days, they would galumph around the garden with our dogs. Nowadays, we provide special enclosures, but sometimes

I cannot help feeling that our visitors miss the occasional otter biting one of their wellies!

Schweppes and You Know Who were our first breeding pair. They were North American otters and, in 1972, You Know Who presented us with three handsome cubs. You Know Who proved to be an excellent mother, if aggressive towards the other otters while she was with the cubs. The nest was always immaculately clean. She carried each cub out to go to the loo, and continually fussed over all three of them. Swimming lessons began when the cubs reached nine weeks, with paddling sessions at first, slowly progressing to the deep end. Surprisingly, young otters swim badly at first, and Mother plays an essential role as life-guard.

Schweppes was allowed to return to his family when the cubs were about five months old. Schweppes loved his parental role, and invented all sorts of games for his young family to play. Eventually the cubs were found good homes and life returned to normal. Schweppes and You Know Who returned to the enclosure they had always shared with Beady Eyes and Needle Teeth, a pair of smooth-coated Indian otters.

Schweppes and You Know Who bred regularly—but when their last litter was about three months old, disaster struck. All the adults were hit by a fatal bacterium, which only Schweppes survived.

Jaws, Snap and Scrunch, the cubs, had therefore to be hand-reared. Their names are perfectly descriptive and to say they wreaked havoc would be a complete understatement. Thankfully, however, rearing the cubs took up so much of our time that it helped ease the sorrow of losing the other otters. We kept Snap for breeding and eventually she produced four cubs, who were particularly extrovert and, because they were very approachable and gregarious, were often the subjects of paintings and sculptures.

In 1982, we decided to introduce some wild North American otters to the collection in order to ensure that we did not suffer from the problems caused by interbreeding related animals. Rapid and Spray, the males, and Missouri joined us after a considerable search.

Everyday life with the otters brings much to amuse and fascinate us—they are all such individual personalities. At times, we have spotted an otter swimming around with the lens of some poor visitor's spectacles balanced on its nose. Nothing gives them greater pleasure than to play with humans' mysterious belongings which accidentally fall into their enclosure. Cameras can provide hours of interest, but babies' bootees are torn to bits in seconds! Otters are inextricably involved in our life and I am sure that it would be a much duller, although sometimes quieter, existence without them.

SIMON HICKS

Jambo
The Gentle Giant of Jersey

JERSEY WILDLIFE
PRESERVATION TRUST

S unday, 31 August 1986; three-fifty p.m.; Jersey Wildlife Preservation Trust. Five-year-old Levan Merrit lay motionless in the gorilla enclosure. His father had lifted him over the safety barrier on to the perimeter wall of the enclosure. He had then turned away to pick up a second child to join his son. The little boy stood up, lost his balance, toppled three and a half metres, and landed head first on the concrete water drain at the base of the gorillas' enclosure, sustaining a fractured skull and a broken arm.

Jambo and his family of three wives, N'Pongo, Nandi and Kishka, with their young, Motaba, Rafiki and two-month-old Sakina (Swahili for 'happy family'), were some forty-five metres away waiting to go indoors for afternoon tea. The sound of a human 'alarm call', coming from one of the watching members of the public, alerted Jambo, who immediately set off to investigate, followed closely by the family. Without showing any sign of aggression at all, Jambo straddled the unconscious child and sniffed him all over, touching him gently and discovering that he was bleeding. He firmly shouldered his nearest wife, Nandi, out of the way and placed himself between the rest of the family and the boy. He then sat quietly and looked up at the spectators to see what was being done.

Exactly four minutes from the time of the fall, the child began to come round, cried and moved. Although Levan has no recollection of the incident, to observers he appeared to look at Jambo. The boy's distress seemed to upset the gorilla, who quickly decided to take his family back to the building where the animal staff had made preparations for their immediate entry.

In order to let Jambo's family enter, Hobbit, an adolescent male from Zurich, had to be allowed access to the enclosure. Hobbit was as interested in the strange events as Jambo, and immediately raced over towards the boy, arriving just before Andy Wood, staff assistant of the great ape section. Fortunately, Hobbit and Andy have a very good relationship, and so Andy felt confident that he could control the young gorilla without much difficulty. Even so, although there was little danger to the child, Hobbit's typically arrogant stance and posturing must have looked more threatening to the onlookers than Jambo's gentle and concerned approach. A second member of the staff and an ambulance crew member dropped into the enclosure precisely eleven minutes after the fall. The keeper remained with Andy, keeping Hobbit's natural exuberance at a safe distance, while the ambulanceman was safely lifted out of the enclosure with Levan.

Although the accident was unfortunate, the operation went quickly and smoothly and the Trust staff were immediately on hand to bring in the gorillas, control the crowd and summon the emergency services. Throughout the incident, Brian Le Lion, a Jerseyman, recorded the event on his video equipment and Peter De Sousa, a college student, took still photographs, all of which circulated the globe, appearing on television news and in national papers. Thankfully, the little boy made a full recovery, and his father publicly took full responsibility for the accident.

The repercussions of the incident, however, continued for many months. Among the first to contact us was David Attenborough. He explained that he was not surprised by Jambo's reaction, having had first-hand experience of the gentleness of the mountain gorilla in the wild during the production of his

Below: *When Levan Merrit fell into the gorilla enclosure at Jersey Zoo, Jambo carefully guarded the boy. He then sat quietly and looked up at the spectators to see what was being done. Right: Jambo, 'the gentle giant'.*

famous TV series 'Life on Earth'. By managing species in a way which allows their natural interrelationships to develop, it would seem from this incident that the true nature of the animal can be preserved.

Jambo was heralded as 'the gentle giant'. Fan mail poured in from every corner of the world, addressed not to the Trust staff, but to Jambo himself. From children came their pocket money, old-age pensioners sent in what they could and even the American Army sent a donation! Pounds of bananas were sent to Jambo, as were carefully composed verses, an example of which came from four hard-working mums at Electrolux, Luton:

> A little boy you did save
> From terror and danger, you're so brave
> The other gorillas you kept at bay
> So the four of us would like to say
> Thank you Jambo! Hip! Hip! Hooray!

Jambo was so touched by this that he commissioned his resident scribe to respond on his behalf:

> It's very kind of you to praise me
> But all this fussing does amaze me
> If my boy fell into your zoo
> You would try to help him too.

He also received a postcard from his sister Quarta at Basle Zoo, who conveyed love and praises from his mother Achilla, one of his sons, Tamtam, and various nieces and nephews.

One of the nicest compliments paid to Jambo, however, was by the BBC's *Wildlife Magazine*, which announced the institution of a new award. A splendidly inscribed certificate has now arrived at the Wildlife Preservation Trust and reads as follows:

> This is to commemorate the instigation of the Jambo Award in honour of Jambo, the silver-back lowland gorilla, resident of the Jersey Wildlife Preservation Trust. The Award will consist of £100 to be given by BBC *Wildlife Magazine*, annually, to a suitable wildlife or conservation charity in honour of the individual animal which, in the view of the readers of the magazine, has done most to make humans more aware of the true nature and/or needs of the other animal species with which we share the world.

Jambo's approval was sought and readily given for the first £100 to be sent to the Digit Fund, established by the late Diane Fossey in memory of her equally famous wild mountain gorilla who suffered such a dreadful end at the hands of poachers.

By his action, Jambo has probably done more for the reputation of his species than any other recorded event.

The Saga of Saga

THE ZOOLOGICAL SOCIETY
OF WALES

There is a good westerly breeze and, simply by opening his wings, Saga the eagle is lifted from his hilltop perch. Keeping his head into the breeze and with instinctive minor adjustments to his wings and tail, he makes a beautifully controlled ascent. The rush of wind over the upper surface of his wings gives him all the lift he needs; scarcely a flap of them is required. Up twenty-five, fifty, a hundred metres above the hilltop!

To his right, a hundred metres below, is the familiar sight of his take off point. What he sees would no doubt prove alarming to a wild eagle, but to Saga it is a reassuring and attractive sight. At the top of the wooded hill, known for a hundred years as the Flagstaff, is an open area. Here, gathered in a semi-circle, are over five hundred people. They are watching Saga. They are seeing, perhaps for the first time in their lives, the incredible flight of an eagle. Within the semi-circle is a lone figure with one gloved fist upraised. Saga knows what the glove means; he can also see what it contains. With an eyesight probably seven or eight times better than a man's, he easily detects the small piece of meat in the glove. Reassuring himself that the person on the other end of the arm is the trainer that he knows and trusts, Saga prepares to dive. To the crowd below, he appears to be hanging on the wind, not moving at all. As they watch, the wings, spanning two metres when open, partially close and without their lift Saga starts to fall. In the space of three seconds, he is breaking the speed of his descent and making a well-controlled landing, talons outstretched, on the trainer's fist. No sooner has he devoured the meat than Saga is off again.

Saga is a wedgetailed eagle. Although it is an a Australian species, home for Saga is the wooded hilltop in North Wales that he sees below him as he flies—the Welsh Mountain Zoo at Colwyn Bay. If he knew just where to look down among the trees, he would be able to see his parents in their aviary and perhaps even make out the nest where he started life as an egg. He would also detect the incubation room where on 26 March 1982 he emerged from the egg.

No mother hen could have clucked and fussed more assiduously, nor any expectant father paced more nervously than head keeper Lee Thomas at the time of Saga's hatching. From the moment the first crack appeared in the shell to his final emergence from the egg was a period of great tension for the keeping staff. Should the hatching chick be helped? All expert advice seemed to be that if a chick needs help to hatch it will probably not survive anyway. In the end, as is so often the case, success resulted from striking the right balance between standing back and letting nature take its course, and stepping in and giving the minimum of assistance where required. What emerged from the egg was the kind of damp, wrinkled little blob with which only a mother, or a zoo keeper, could fall in love.

The transformation of this unlikely little creature weighing barely a hundred grams to the beautiful three-kilogram eagle capable of displaying the most incredible aerobatic ability, was one of the wonders of nature. Only once previously, in East Berlin Zoo, had this species been bred in captivity outside Australia. Every stage of Saga's development was recorded. Plots, charts and graphs were drawn. He was weighed, measured and photographed. Of course, great care was taken to ensure that nothing disturbed the developing eaglet. His food intake increased from just a few grammes of chicken a day when newly hatched to sometimes over five hundred grammes of beef and chicken a day when he was sixty days old. By ten weeks old, Saga was certainly looking the part—an unmistakable eagle. He was moved to a large, indoor enclosure where he would sit on his low perch trying to look grown-up. To the experienced eye, his light, reddish-brown plumage was the most obvious indication of his youth. An adult wedgetailed eagle sports plumage of a very dark brown, almost black colour. Even an inexperienced observer could not fail to notice an occasional tiny, white feather still sticking to Saga's head and back, all that remained of his downy baby feathers. Perhaps the biggest give-away of his age was when he tried, with casual nonchalance, to scratch the back of his head with one foot. This is perfectly normal eagle behaviour, but for young Saga it required a rather better-developed sense of balance and co-ordination than he possessed. The result would almost invariably be a rather ignominious heap of feathers collapsed on the floor.

As the weeks passed, he began to take his first tentative, short flights around his indoor quarters. Autumn was approaching and the zoo staff decided it was time for him to move to one of the outdoor aviaries. Here he could not only improve his powers of flight but also for the first time meet other eagles. He was put with two young tawny eagles, and all three birds quickly settled down quite happily. This period of living with the eagles was considered very important for Saga's development. If he was ever to become a breeding adult, he had to learn to associate with other eagles. So, for four years, he lived undisturbed in the aviary with his companions.

Then, one morning in early spring, Saga was moved to a small area in the

Right: *Saga is a wedgetailed eagle who regularly delights his audiences with aerial displays over the wooded hilltop of the Welsh Mountain Zoo.*

zoo known as the mews, where trained birds of prey are kept. He was fitted with a smart pair of leather straps, or jesses as they are known, one on each leg, in the ancient falconry manner and training was begun by bird keeper Melanie Gilbert. Our eagle proved a very willing student and in a matter of just six weeks he had learned to return to Melanie's gloved fist to receive his food. At first, these short flights were on a line, or creance as falconers call it, but soon he was ready for his first free flight. He was, at this time, well capable of good controlled flight in the still, sheltered conditions of his aviary. But up on the hilltop, on the flying arena, controlled flight required skills and muscular fitness that Saga just did not possess. What must at first have looked like a very simple flight, perhaps thirty metres from a perch to the glove, suddenly became a challenging exercise as he found it necessary to cope with cross-winds, up currents, eddies and gusts.

As the weeks went by, Saga's flying skills developed well; there were still the occasional mishaps, however. On one occasion he miscalculated his flying speed as he came in to land on the glove. He knew that he could not safely hit the fist at that speed and so, very sensibly, he overshot and landed on the ground beyond. What he did not realise was that he had landed in the ostrich enclosure. As he stood in the grass trying to regain his composure, he was suddenly confronted by the largest, most amazing-looking birds he had ever seen in his life: two ostriches stood looking down at the cheeky intruder. For Saga, discretion was the better part of valour and he slowly sidled away from between the menacing pair of giants. His walk broke into a trot and then he spread his wings and was away. Zoo staff never knew who was more relieved as he returned to the fist, Saga or Melanie.

For the eagle, these adventures were all part of getting to know his new-found home territory. As his confidence increased, so the distances covered during his flights became greater. Saga is now a superb specimen, strong and fit and with highly developed flying skills. He has a confidence and ability in the air approaching that of a wild eagle and, as his wings start to close and he descends to meet his public, we cannot help but think that his adventures have only just started.

NIGEL MARTIN

Pringle—a Star is Born

CHESSINGTON WORLD OF ADVENTURE

C omedian and television personality Tom O'Connor froze in his chair. For the first time in his professional career he was speechless, too afraid even to breathe. Little wonder—a six-inch pointed beak rested on the top of his thigh!

The owner of this potentially lethal weapon was Pringle, a magnificent king penguin and acclaimed star of 'The Russell Harty Show' on TV. Quite how a bird came to be such a show stopper is a long story, but one thing is certain—there may be thirteen different species of penguin, but there is only one Pringle! He had come to Chessington from Stockholm, and, during the statutory quarantine period, had formed a close and binding relationship with Ron Eaton, the zoo's head keeper. Pringle was unlike any other penguin Ron had encountered; far from being apprehensive of people, he was friendly and indeed actively sought human company.

When he was eventually transferred to the penguin pool, Pringle behaved in a totally unexpected manner. He showed absolutely no interest in the other birds, instead preferring to stand at the edge of the enclosure 'talking' to visitors. At feeding time he would insist upon personal service, standing next to the keeper waiting to be hand-fed, and accepting only the very best fish. But, worst of all— Pringle refused to swim!

A penguin which hated water was an unprecedented and serious problem. Ron knew that for the sake of the bird's health, Pringle had to swim. Penguins are designed to be swimmers. They are perfectly adapted to an aquatic lifestyle. Although they can look quite comical on land, their stunted wings become wonderful flippers to steer them through the water. Their streamlined bodies reduce water resistance and those webbed feet propel them at great speed. Even their feathers, which look so different from those of other birds, have a special purpose: below the skin is a thick layer of blubber which helps keep the penguin warm, but in particularly cold weather the bird will fluff out its feathers, trapping a layer of air next to its skin for extra insulation.

Pringle was definitely in prime condition and the problem could not be that the water was too cold, nor that he could not swim—he simply did not want to! The obvious solution seemed to be for Ron to lead the way into the water and teach by example. But Ron's strange reluctance to follow this course of action was soon explained—Ron could not swim! This latest obstacle was removed by his investing in a pair of waders. But no matter how long Ron stood thigh-deep in water, coaxing Pringle to follow, the penguin would walk to the pool's edge and stubbornly refuse to go one step further.

Desperate measures were called for! Ron, now at his wits' end, resorted to his final solution—to throw Pringle in! Gentle throw though it was, the instant Pringle touched the water, he shot back to shore. Each immersion lasted a mere few seconds, yet twice a day Ron had to 'persuade' Pringle to swim—it was a case of trying to convince him that he enjoyed it.

That is how his rise to celebrity status began. The local TV station heard about the amazing non-swimming penguin and decided to feature him on one of their news programmes. Not only did Pringle refuse to enter the water, but he insisted on meeting personally the entire film crew, walking round the grounds with them and displaying an undeniable acquaintance with film techniques. It seemed as if he knew exactly when the camera was rolling, and walked straight towards it on cue. When 'interviewed' he nodded and shook his head almost as if he understood the questions. The news item received more letters from viewers than any other shown on the programme, and the station had to repeat the clip time and again.

So public demand for Pringle began to grow. First to call was 'The Russell Harty Show'. They were preparing a show to be broadcast live from around film star Diana Dors's swimming-pool, and wanted Pringle to guest alongside Adam Ant, the swimmer Duncan Goodhew, Tom O'Connor, Diana herself, and a specially-selected celebrity audience. Would Pringle be able to do it? Ron Eaton thought he would—at least he did until he was asked whether Pringle would join the guests in a final plunge into the pool! The show's producer simply refused to believe that Pringle really hated water and booked him to appear, in the misguided hope that on the night Pringle would in fact perform.

Transporting the new star presented a further dilemma. Under no circumstances whatsoever would Ron subject the bird to stress—he would not have even contemplated the idea with any 'normal' penguin. But Pringle was proving himself no normal penguin, showing a distinct propensity for human company and for being the centre of human attention. What was soon apparent, however, was that Pringle positively despised being treated as—a penguin! Just seeing the penguin-carrying crate induced in him a dreadful fit of temperament. He puffed and panted to such an extent that Ron was just about to cancel the trip. Then suddenly, quite unprompted and with singular perversity, Pringle walked straight up the loading ramp and into the waiting estate car. There he stood, patiently waiting for his chauffeur.

From then on, that is exactly how he travelled, standing in the back of the car watching the traffic and people go by. Passing drivers could not believe their eyes. Some tried to ignore this vision, perhaps assuming that he was not

Right: *Pringle, the penguin who wouldn't swim.*

real, or was maybe a figment of their imagination. Others gasped in stunned amazement.

On arrival, Pringle obliged with two perfect rehearsals, calmly greeting the guests and coping with the situation like a real professional. Ron's only concern was keeping him cool, which was achieved with the help of Diana's shower-room!

On air! All Pringle had to do was, as rehearsed, to walk down one side of Diana's pool and straight off the set. But even greater fame beckoned! Our star walked on as rehearsed, then confidently turned and planted himself centre stage, right between Tom O'Connor's legs, his beak resting coolly on the poor man's thigh. And he refused to budge! Pringle hogged the screen for a full ten minutes, until a suitable break enabled Ron to persuade him to exit stage left—and allowed the relieved Mr O'Connor to take several very deep breaths.

From that performance, Pringle went on to star in numerous programmes, regularly rubbing shoulders with the rich and famous—even appearing on a radio programme, which, as he never uttered a sound, must have been quite scintillating entertainment! When working, particularly for the BBC, Pringle had his own contracts, which stipulated that he be provided with his own dressing room and shower, privileges normally afforded only to the highest-paid stars. And, in order to comply with union regulations, he received the Equity fee equivalent to that of a walk-on, non-speaking actor!

Pringle is still at Chessington and has finally been convinced that swimming is not the undignified activity he at first thought, and he now regularly takes the plunge unaided. Nothing else about him has changed, however, and he remains a highly unusual bird. Many people find it hard to believe that he has never been trained, but coaching prospective television personalities has never been a consideration of the staff at Chessington, where the main priorities continue to be the welfare of animals and the conservation of rare and endangered species. Pringle the king penguin is a unique creature, a bird with a charming personality who has won the hearts of Chessington staff, visitors and stars alike.

JOHN KNOWLES

Sire Basil
The Noblest of Stallions

MARWELL ZOOLOGICAL PARK

B asil, whose full name was Catskill Basil, came to Marwell in 1969. He had previously been alone in a collection of various members of the horse family belonging to a dentist from Kentucky and, as was evident from my research, was one of the very few Przewalski stallions in the world of a particularly important lineage. The breed became extinct in the wild in the 1950s and unless zoos throughout the world developed good captive breeding programmes this beautiful animal could be lost for ever. If I wanted to fulfil my aim to establish a worthwhile, genetically-strong group, I had little choice other than to take Basil and find out by trial and error whether he would be a good father. As it turned out, Basil proved to be one of the most genetically-important Przewalskis in the world.

From the very beginning, Basil proved himself a very strong-willed and forceful character who would stand no nonsense from anyone—and that included human beings. He had absolutely no time for us two-legged animals and would seize every opportunity to get the better of us. The keepers learned that bending down to adjust a shoelace or to pick up rubbish anywhere near him was an extremely tricky exercise, and they risked two teeth-shaped bruises on their buttocks if they were not careful. Basil was usually much kinder to the general public. However, for some totally unaccountable reason, one day he took objection to a perfectly charming gentleman who was unfortunately bereft of hair.

It was an August Bank Holiday Monday. Of all the thousands of people who must have admired the Przewalskis that day, Basil singled out this bald visitor. Somehow he managed to clamber up on the normally protective fence, rest his forelegs on the top and then sink his teeth into the shiny pate! Luckily for us, the bitten visitor took the incident in very good part and, having had his poor head patched up by my wife, far from suing us, he considered it quite an honour to have been bitten by such a rare creature as a Przewalski's horse!

Another of Basil's tricks was to charge at full speed directly towards any Homo sapiens who, for any accountable reason, offended his sensibilities. One's only form of defence was attack! By standing one's ground, yelling 'Basil' as loudly as possible while holding up a stone and raising one's arm as if about

Beavering Away

DRUSILLA'S ZOO PARK

F rom the moment he was born, Michael Ann, the owner of Drusilla's Zoo in Sussex, has shared his life with animals. His father established Drusilla's in 1925, originally as a tea-room with a pets' corner as an added attraction for visiting families. Eventually, however, the animal side just grew and grew, and Drusilla's became and remains one of the most popular zoos for children in southern England.

Obviously, during its history as a zoo, Drusilla's has changed considerably, reflecting the increased knowledge of the specialised needs of animals and the continually changing educational and recreational requirements of children. During the 1970s, Michael helped to start the Rare Breed Survival Trust and he kept an incredible range of weird and wonderful-looking cattle and sheep, the most memorable of which were the seaweed-eating sheep of North Ronaldsey. These almost wild sheep were traditionally kept outside the sea walls on the Scottish island and survived by putting their heads below the sea water and eating seaweed.

Michael brought an entire herd, including a ram, from Scotland, as he wanted not only to help to preserve this unusual breed, but also to discover whether they adopted this curious diet out of necessity or choice. He placed the wild bunch in his walled garden, where he felt sure that they would be secure. He then informed the local media of this very peculiar breed of sheep, which only ate seaweed. A news crew duly came to film the animals. However, the moment the sheep saw grass, their heads went down and they began eating as if they had never eaten anything else—much to the dismay of the newsmen. They were not to go away without a story, though! Suddenly, before his very eyes, one of the herd ran at the wall, used a jutting piece of flint as a springboard, and cleared it beautifully. Naturally, sheep-like, the others immediately followed. In minutes, the sheep had disappeared into the distance, with Michael and keepers in hot pursuit. The sheep covered four parishes in half an hour, including crossing the railway line just before the four thirty-five p.m. train from Victoria to Eastbourne, and crossing back again before the returning train.

Their second escape coincided with another visit from the local press, after which Michael refused to co-operate with any journalist who wanted to write about the sheep—it was just tempting fate. That was until someone asked if it would be possible to take just one of the sheep down to the beach to discover if it would still eat seaweed, having become accustomed to a different standard of living. It was too tempting an experiment for Michael to refuse and so he agreed to take the ram to Beachy Head. He attached the ram to a version of a fishing reel so that he would not end up chasing the animal for miles over the sands but could just 'reel him in'. As soon as the ram was released, he bolted towards the sea and began swimming in the direction of France. Michael's ingenious 'fishing-reel' was put to the test and, thankfully, worked perfectly, and they were able to haul the ram out of the water with some ease. The fascinating aspect of the beach trip, however, was that the ram now identified some kelp below the water and tucked in as though the seaweed were manna from heaven!

More recently, Drusilla's won the University Federation of Animal Welfare Award for their new and brilliantly-conceived beaver enclosure. Michael felt that these fascinating creatures had been rather overlooked in other British zoos, and that a great deal of research had to be carried out in order to provide better enclosures for them. With this in mind, he began to search for a pair of captive-bred beavers, to discover that there were only seventeen beavers in the entire country! Eventually, Edinburgh Zoo promised him a pair and work began on the new enclosure.

Michael began his research into the perfect beaver home by contacting the Grey Owl Society. This small organisation is named after the crusading Red Indian who, during the 1930s, travelled widely, giving lectures to packed theatres on the conservation of American wildlife. He had begun living as a trapper, but eventually saw the error of his ways and swapped his hunting equipment for a notebook and pencil and so recorded the behaviour of animals in the wild in fascinating detail. Grey Owl was finally discovered to be a fraud since, beneath the impressive head-dress and war paint, was an Englishman, born in Hastings, who was simply masquerading as a Red Indian. However, despite this deception, Grey Owl's work remains some of the most comprehensive on northern American wildlife and Michael based a great deal of his planning on the drawings of lodges and accounts of beaver behaviour which the self-styled Indian compiled.

Through the society, which is based in Hastings, Michael also met a very interested vet who gladly gave him invaluable advice—beginning with doubling the proposed size of both the enclosure and the pools. Unlike any other beaver enclosure, the surface is grassed, despite beavers being renowned for their digging. To overcome the effects of their natural tendency to tunnel, Michael laid wire mesh a few feet below the grass. Perhaps one of the most fascinating aspects of the enclosure is the constantly moving copse! A series of drain-pipes has been planted in the ground and branches of willow are placed in them every evening. The beavers are thus able to fell their own trees, and their enclosure changes its appearance all the time. Such a simple and inexpensive idea helps keep the animals happy and in good mental and physical condition.

Initially, Michael kept one end of the lodge open so that he could observe the beavers inside. However, beavers value their privacy and they quickly wove branches through the open wire mesh, completely blocking off the lodge from prying eyes. The animal beavers are of particular interest to the human variety of little boys who are a sub-species of the cub scouts and meet in colonies. The Beavers has become one of the most popular new organisations for the under-eights. Michael has invited Beavers from all over the South of England to come and view their namesakes and many of the colonies have decided to adopt the beavers, Gnawer and Gnasher.

Michael has now made a visit to Drusilla's both a learning and an entertaining experience, where children, with the help of such inventions as the Geoff Capes Animal Challenge, can discover what it is like as a mongoose to be chased by an eagle, or just how high a serval can jump, and can compare their own ability and mobility with those of the animals.

Below: *A ruffed lemur with a keeper at Drusilla's, one of the most popular zoos for children in southern England.*

Three-Foot Flying Rainbows

THE TROPICAL BIRD GARDENS, RODE

T here is hardly a more beautiful sight, in my opinion, than the macaws flying in from all directions in response to the alluring sound of my husband banging a tin which contains their much-loved shortcake biscuits. 'Three-foot flying rainbows' is a perfect description of the scarlet, blue-and-gold and green-winged macaws as they descend upon our tea lawn, using the bemused visitors' chairs, tables and sometimes even their heads as landing points en route to the source of their favourite treat.

When we bought the land to create the Tropical Bird Gardens in 1961, it was more like a jungle than a potential home for the breeding and rearing of rare and endangered birds. However, having cleared reed-covered swamps and terribly overgrown ponds, we were able to introduce the first birds, which included the blue-and-gold macaws Raucous, Rodney, Rosy and Lofty. Raucous and Rodney were our first birds to breed, which was a bit of a surprise to us, as we had thought that Rodney was a male!

In those days it was almost impossible correctly to sex the birds and many 'pairs' turned out to be 'just good friends'. Today, we can define their gender surgically by using a laparoscope, which enables us to ensure that each of the pairs is actually male and female and saves me having continually to explain why we have a hen bird called Rodney!

Lofty provided another case of mistaken sexuality! For several years we referred to her as a him, and only discovered our mistake when 'he' laid eggs! Lofty acquired 'his' name from 'his' tendency to fly to the top of our highest fir trees, only to find that 'he' couldn't get down again! 'He' would let everyone know of 'his' predicament by filling the air with screams of 'Awwo' and 'Whoaw', no doubt macaw-ese for, 'Anybody there . . . please help!' Once located, Lofty had to be talked down. 'He' had to be coaxed and coached every step of 'his' descent, each successful negotiation being celebrated by 'his' squeals of delight. When 'he' settled on the lower branches, these sessions would only take a few

Previous page: *A scarlet macaw called Edwina had a strange affinity with people. It was uncanny how she seemed to know when something was wrong.*

hours, but the nearer the top of the tree 'he' flew the longer they took—sometimes days!

Rosy and Lofty also acted as weather forecasters. Somehow, they always knew when it was about to rain and could be seen making their way across the lawns to the gift shop, where they would remain happily until the weather improved. Lofty was a tame macaw and could easily be handled, as long as no one took any liberties. Because she had such a pleasant personality, she appeared on many television programmes. However, many of the early performances were somewhat marred by her penchant for disappearing from the perch and performing acrobatics behind the studio scenery the minute the cameras were directed on her!

Another of our remarkable characters was a scarlet macaw called Edwina, a bird donated to us by a family called Edwards—hence the name. Edwina needed to be near humans, but unfortunately developed uncontrollable likes and dislikes. She absolutely delighted in terrorising the objects of her hatred. After such attacks she had to be removed perched on a broom handle and quickly returned to an aviary. Despite this erratic behaviour, she had a strange affinity with people and would fly to our house to knock on the window, especially when someone was ill or had been away from the bird gardens for a time. It was uncanny how she seemed to know when something was wrong. One day she came knocking at the window and none of us could think why—we had all been at home and everyone was in good health. The next morning we discovered that she had died during the night. Could she have been saying her final goodbye? I like to think so.

Then there was the beastly Beppo, a blue-and-gold macaw, who at first seemed a gentle, kindly bird. Then he developed a sudden aversion to spectacles and, in particular, to mine! He would 'lie in wait', then dive-bomb me in a flurry of blue and gold feathers. It was a terrifying experience! I became adept at Beppo-dodging and could spot him from yards away and would charge for cover if there was any chance of being subjected to one of his baffling bombings.

It appears to be quite a regular phenomenon for a macaw suddenly to develop irrational dislikes. We have been given many birds who, after a happy co-existence within a family, have suddenly taken a grudge against the wife or husband for no accountable reason. It inevitably results in one or other of them issuing an 'it's me or that bird' ultimatum, and so the offending marauder ends up at the Tropical Bird Gardens.

In the twenty-six years that the gardens have been in existence, we have successfully bred over three hundred macaws and continue to work with all the species, particularly those which have proved difficult to rear in captivity and whose numbers are decreasing in the wild.

KIM SIMMONS

Quasimodo Gets His Esmeralda

LINTON ZOOLOGICAL GARDENS

Quasimodo knew what a life without love meant. He had lived alone for over twelve years without the joy and affection that only a partner can bring. But who could love the hump-backed giant whose skin was armour-plated and whose stumpy legs barely lifted him from the ground? Only another of the same kind could possibly feel true and honest affection for him, but where on earth would he find another African giant spurred tortoise in Cambridgeshire?

Of course, there were plenty of others who cared deeply about him, who looked after him and made sure that his every need was catered for. But there was one area in which, care as they might, they could never fully compensate for the missing link in his otherwise complete life—a wife. Poor Quasimodo seemed doomed to his solitary existence!

Kim Simmons had acquired him for Linton Zoo in the belief that it would be easy to find him a partner. As with all their animals, the Simmons family, which owns and runs the park, naturally wanted Quasimodo to have a mate. They tried on his behalf to find a solitary female who would appreciate the attentions of their lonely male, only to discover that there was only one other of the species in the country, and that also was a male. The country of origin has an exportation ban on the species. This is strictly adhered to, even though, as Kim discovered to her horror, the tortoises are used for target practice by some of the less scrupulous military!

Despite Kim's assiduous care, feeding Quasimodo with his favourite titbits, scavenging through the hedgerows for the particular wild herbs which he liked and constantly ensuring that his environment was always warm enough, she knew that Quasimodo's life would not be complete without a female. Neither would her work, if she did not try to breed the giant tortoises.

After many years, Kim received some wonderful news from her friends in Florida who specialised in breeding rare and endangered species. Kim and her sister Dawn had visited Florida the previous year and had mentioned that she was urgently looking for a female African spurred tortoise. Little did she expect that her American friends would remember Quasimodo's plight and would also come up trumps. The fantastic news was that they had found him not just one female—but two! They were simply waiting to be flown over the Atlantic to cheer up Quasimodo's solitary life.

As always with true love, however, nothing comes that easy! The problem was created by the country of origin. The females had originally come from Togo, although they had lived in Florida Zoo for many years. On the import licence, it was necessary to specify the precise country of birth. So, according to procedure, Kim wrote 'Togo'. When the Department of the Environment officials checked in their reference books, they discovered that the African giant spurred tortoise did not live in Togo and therefore the tortoises could not have come from there. Despite the experts' opinions which confirmed Kim's information, the bureaucrats refused to budge. So Kim had to pretend that they

Below: *Quasimodo and Esmeralda, two African giant spurred tortoises in love.*

came from Cameroon, just to keep the officials happy. Meanwhile, in the United States, the equivalent export licence was being completed and, naturally, the Americans supplied the correct country of origin.

The two females had now become the centre of world-wide press attention. Their journey to meet the lovelorn Quasimodo had captured the imagination of newsmen from as far afield as Japan and Australia. Esmeralda, the larger tortoise, was the object of their particular interest. Would this Esmeralda not only be saved by Quasimodo, but, in contradiction of the original story of *The Hunchback of Notre Dame*, stay with him and live happily ever after?

British Airways had sponsored their flight home through their Assisting Nature Conservation Project. And so, the two animals were to be given VIP treatment, travelling in a specially-designed flight-crate, and accompanied for the entire journey by an airways representative, to ensure that they were comfortable throughout the journey and that their every need would be satisfied.

Back in Britain, however, things were not running so smoothly. The hawk-eyed officials had noticed the discrepancy between import and export licences and had refused to allow the tortoises to come into Heathrow until it was sorted out. There were only two days to go. The Simmons family had been arranging the details of this tortoise transportation for months, and its members were just about at the end of their tether.

When Kim eventually turned in exasperation to her father and told him that it looked as though Quasimodo would never have a mate, Len Simmons could stand no more. He got on to the 'phone and absolutely refused to hang up until he was assured that the matter would be sorted out once and for all that very day; otherwise he would go personally with Quasimodo to the Department of the Environment and sort the matter out for himself! Such a threat worked like magic. Obviously the proposition of a tortoise protesting in the ministry was more than the officials could contemplate! An emergency meeting was held and within two hours they had agreed that the tortoises could come into the country, so that Kim could start the breeding programme which she had been working on with her Florida counterparts. So Esmeralda and her as yet unnamed friend finally boarded the flight to Britain.

When they arrived at Linton, the welcoming committee of news reporters was as large as the farewell party. The big question was, how would Quasimodo take to the females? Would he, as the story goes, love and protect Esmeralda? And would she reciprocate?

As it was, he pretended to show little interest at first, and the three animals, once introduced, walked in separate directions, taking no notice of each other! It soon became apparent, however, that all three were happily ensconced in their home, with the two females taking full advantage of the lush green grass and the clover which they could not get in such plentiful supply in their original home. However, there was one last problem—what to call the third tortoise. It was solved by the flood of correspondence created by the national news coverage. Almost every letter suggested the name Belle!

KAREN KADI

Breakfast at Timothy's

ROBIN HILL COUNTRY PARK

T he young press photographer gingerly dipped his fingers into the carton of apricot yoghurt and extricated his camera lens-cover with disgust. His other hand was protecting his one spare roll of film, which looked precariously close to suffering the same fate.

The young subject of the photographer's interest, Timothy, surveyed the chaos he had created with apparent delight. This morning's breakfast was certainly proving to be far more entertaining than usual. The tiny monkey paused for a second and began sucking his thumb in a child-like gesture of contentment. But he darted away the instant he noticed the hand of his surrogate mother moving in his direction to try and control him.

Alison Benton, who had taken on the responsibility for the upbringing of this wayward baby, apologetically offered wads of tissues to the yoghurt-splattered photographer while endeavouring to bring a sense of order back to the proceedings. 'Oh I am sorry,' she repeated for the umpteenth time that morning. 'He does so enjoy his breakfasts.' She laughed and finally managed to take a firm grip on the mischievous crab-eating macaque to whom she had become mother. Timothy curled up in Alison's arms like a human baby and glared balefully at the photographer who, by that time, had placed all his expensive photographic equipment well out of the reach of the curious monkey.

Timothy, or 'Tiny Tim' as the local press had aptly named him, was born on 14 November 1986, weighing in at just half a kilo. His mother, Vicky, had shown absolutely no interest in her offspring, and so, to ensure his survival, Timothy had to be adopted. Alison had originally joined Robin Hill Adventure Park on a Youth Training Scheme but, after three years, was still there looking after the monkeys. Under the close supervision of Jon Buck, she became Timothy's foster-mother, which soon proved an enormous responsibility.

Being so tiny, Timothy required constant nourishment to help maintain his body temperature. That meant two-hourly feeds—night and day! Alison diligently took on this daunting task, bottle-feeding him with powdered baby milk. It is doubtful whether even a monkey mother could have devoted such care and attention to her baby. Nappy changing was a similarly arduous routine, though necessary as Timothy was living at Alison's home and she did not relish the idea of her belongings being covered with monkey droppings. Her boyfriend used to help, which was the only way she could get some sleep. She still had duties at the zoo to carry out and therefore needed to be able to rest sometimes!

Alison carried Timothy around with her all the time, making sure that he could not get up to mischief and, more importantly, ensuring that he was warm and comfortable. At night, he had his own play-pen, complete with his very own cuddly toys. He even had tiny knitted vests personally tailored to fit his minute body, which made sure that he kept warm throughout the night. After the nappy-changing routine was bath-time. A female monkey spends hours cleaning and grooming her baby and so Alison tried to imitate this by bathing Timothy daily. This was not a straightforward procedure, however, nor without its adventures. Soap, in particular, was a major fascination for Timothy and bubbles provided endless fun. He loved to blow them for himself and even seemed to enjoy the soapy taste in his mouth. From being initially a reluctant aquatic, Timothy very soon became a bath-time fanatic and it could take ages to persuade him to leave the water. Crab-eating macaques, as their name implies, would have naturally taken to water at some stage in their development in order to catch the crustaceans which form part of their diet.

As Timothy grew, he developed certain likes and dislikes. He much enjoyed travelling in the car, for instance. For obvious reasons of safety, Alison tried to keep Timothy in a small cage when on journeys, but he soon made it known that he much preferred to sit in the passenger seat next to the driver. He won Alison's confidence by sitting very still and watching out of the window throughout the entire journey, so she gave in and added the role of personal chauffeuse to a crab-eating macaque to her ever-increasing list of responsibilities.

Eventually Timothy was introduced to a foster-mother called Mandy, an elderly macaque who was very experienced in rearing wayward youngsters. The two became friends immediately and Mandy fulfilled her role with aplomb, despite being constantly harassed by Timothy's boisterous antics.

Timothy is one of the most popular animals at Robin Hill Adventure Park and still enjoys the company of humans. In particular, he has never forgotten the attention of the local journalist and every time he sees a camera he obligingly turns somersaults for the photographer, as always making himself the centre of attention.

Right: *Crab-eating macaques may look innocent enough, but they can cause chaos at meal-times.*

LEE THOMAS

My Blunders with Black Basil

COLCHESTER ZOO

B asil is a binturong, or, as it is often known, a bear cat. He and his mate Brenda had arrived at my zoo in January 1987. They were both quite young and so I kept them under constant supervision during their first weeks in their new home. They took great pleasure in exploring their new environment. Not a square centimetre was left uninvestigated. Once they had accomplished this to their satisfaction, they settled down happily.

Therefore, you can imagine my concern when, one day in March, I went to see them both, only to discover young Basil almost motionless in his straw. The inquisitive young animal, who only the day before had been full of mischief, remained quietly sleeping all day. Something was obviously very wrong. I checked his temperature, to discover that it was very low. By now he appeared practically lifeless. It was exactly at that moment that I made the fateful decision. I lifted Basil out of his bed and carried him carefully to my own house, where I thought I would be able to keep a better watch on him. That was *mistake number one!*

The vet came to the house in the middle of the night. He gave Basil a thorough check-up and injected him with antibiotics. Not being completely sure of the cause of the illness, the vet also took some blood samples and smears for further analysis at his laboratory. The best advice he could give me was to keep Basil warm. He said that he would return in the morning.

I transferred Basil to a snug position next to the radiator in my own bedroom. That was *mistake number two*. Mind you, at the time he was so poorly that I could hardly have made any other choice. He had to be hand-fed every two hours and would only take the smallest amount of warm milk from a teaspoon. The rest of the time he simply slept—and I simply did not!

The results of the laboratory tests threw no light on the matter and we concluded that Basil was suffering from a virus. It took a worrying, sleepless week before I detected any signs of Basil's recovery. Slowly his appetite returned. To begin with, he ate small pieces of banana and then his intake of liquid greatly increased. I was delighted to watch him eating again, and encouraged him to take more and more. Little did I realise that my pleasure at his regaining of appetite would soon become a dread of his seemingly insatiable desire for food. That makes *mistake number three*.

Nevertheless, at this time I was pleased with his progress. He was beginning to take short walks around my bedroom and would lie on my bed while I fed him. It seemed a good idea at the time; after all, it saved me having to get up in the middle of the night to feed him! Naturally, he became used to sharing the bed and I rather enjoyed having him with me. That was *mistake number four*.

People are supposed to learn from their mistakes, but at this stage of Basil's convalescence I was blissfully unaware that I had made any. So when I was woken by a loud bang in the middle of the night, accompanied by music blasting out at full volume and a frantic banging I was, not surprisingly, scared out of my wits!

Rubbing my eyes and clearing my head as quickly as possible, I saw Basil with the cord of my bedside lamp around his neck frantically trying to escape and, in so doing, banging the lamp against the wall! As I looked around the room, things became a little clearer. His decision to join me in the middle of the night had obviously resulted in a cataclysmic series of events. First, he had accidentally trodden on the remote control of the television, setting it off at full volume. The blast had so frightened him that he had bolted and knocked my radio on to the ground —hence the crash. And finally, he had ended up inextricably caught up in the flex of the lamp. All this because I had encouraged him to join me in bed!

Binturongs are omnivorous, that is to say they will eat anything, and as Basil grew in strength he constantly provided living proof of an omnivore's wide and varied diet. Friday night is my only opportunity to get the week's food supply and so having carefully pulled out the plugs to the television and lamp, and made sure that there was nothing he could knock over, I locked Basil in my bedroom, knowing that I would only be away for a short while.

Basil was fast asleep when I arrived back with my arms full of groceries. I left the bedroom door open as I carefully loaded the fridge with my week's supply of food. Then I went to bed. I awoke at five thirty a.m. slightly less alert than usual and, when I left home to tend to my elephants, I completely forgot about Basil. *Mistake number five*.

In my absence Basil had woken up—hungry as usual! So he went off in search of food. His hunt led him downstairs and into the kitchen. It did not take long before his powerful sense of smell led him to the fridge and, using his long claws, he carefully opened the door!

When I got home at about nine thirty a.m. I was confronted by total devastation! All my eggs had been smashed and eaten. Two pieces of prime rump steak had been devoured. Gone were my bacon, liver, sausages, butter. Even the frozen fish fingers had disappeared! Nothing had escaped, not even the canned food. Unable to gain easy access, the intruder had torn off every label, leaving me with no idea which was beans or spaghetti or peaches!

Where was he? It could only be Basil! I was livid! I found him quite easily—

fast asleep with an overfat belly. All I could think of to keep me calm was that it would only be a few days before he went back with Brenda.

A day or so later, while I was working with the sea-lions in front of rather a large crowd of visitors, I became aware of laughter spreading gradually through the crowd. It was obviously not about anything I was doing and so I turned and asked a lady close by what was causing all the amusement. Apparently, someone had overheard a message on my two-way radio, at the time in a pocket of my jacket, which was hanging on a nearby fence. The message, which had been subtly disguised, ran something like: in a house belonging to a chap called Lee there was a chap called Basil hanging out of the window with a pair of underpants on his head!

I dropped everything and raced to the scene of the crime.

It was as if I had been burgled by the worst of vandals! All my drawers had been tipped upside down, clothes were spread all over the floor—nothing had been left untouched. Also, in his effort to get out on to the window ledge, he had managed to tear down the curtains. Unaware of the damage he had caused yet again, Basil sat blissfully snoozing on the ledge, bathed by the afternoon sun. His thick black coat was glistening and my Y-fronts were round his neck.

Below: *Warning! Binturongs can seriously damage your home.*

After all this, believe me, I learnt! Before I ever left Basil alone again, I implemented a strict regime of preventative measures:

1 Hide everything that may attract his attention.
2 Lock all my suitcases, boxes and cabinets.
3 Put all trousers and shirts in the bathroom and lock the door.
4 Pull all plugs from their sockets.
5 Remove the stereo and television.
6 Tie rope around the fridge and chest of drawers.

By sticking rigidly to this routine I felt sure that even he could not get up to anything. That was my *final mistake!*

There was one treasured item of clothing I had completely forgotten about— my superb pair of hand-made, suede boots. I had often boasted about these beautiful shoes, explaining to admiring fans that they came from Germany and were unique. They do say pride comes before fall, and fell I did, as I returned home to find a thirty-kilogram Basil binturong in his box sleeping soundly, and undoubtedly comfortably, on my magnificent boots.

I gave up!

JOHN STRONG

See the Sea-lions

CITY OF BELFAST ZOO

C alifornian sea-lions are naturally curious and, whether they are in the wild or in captivity, will carefully investigate anything or anyone with whom they come into contact. Their inquisitiveness is generally an endearing feature and people delight at being in such close proximity to wild animals. But, to others, this agreeable trait makes the sea-lions vulnerable.

It was this vulnerability which caused four Californian sea-lions to be moved from their native waters to Belfast, where they now live in the zoo's exciting new enclosure.

Throughout May and June 1983, volunteers from the Californian Marine Mammals Center based at Main Headlands, just outside San Francisco, received distressing 'phone calls from members of the general public, all of whom had sighted three sea-lions who appeared to be stranded. Such consistent information had to be investigated, and so rescuers were despatched to the location. As they approached the sea-lions, it became obvious that all was not well with the animals. Carefully, they were transported back to the Marine Mammals Center and examined by the veterinary consultant. His report revealed just how callously and cruelly human beings can behave.

Someone had exploited the friendly nature of the sea-lions by using them as shooting targets. They must have been swimming around local fishing or pleasure boats, when someone fired at them, filling their heads with shot pellets! The result of this heartless action was that the animals were permanently blind.

The sea-lions were given sanctuary at the Marine Mammals Center, where, with skilful veterinary treatment and nursing, they survived their brutal injuries. The male was christened Chariot, and the females Azul and Arseno. Arseno was particularly badly injured, and X-rays revealed that she had forty-two pieces of shot embedded in her head and neck. Fortunately, they do not seem to cause her any problems, and four years later, with the lead still in her body, she is fit and well.

The principal objective of the Californian establishment is to re-habilitate marine mammals, and then release them back into the wild. The blind sea-lions created quite a dilemma. They obviously would not survive in the wild, and so the release of Chariot, Azul and Arseno was out of the question. At about the same time, Belfast Zoo was putting the finishing touches to its new sea-lion enclosure. Its design and construction were revolutionary, providing the sea-lions with crystal-clear, filtered water, beaches and islands, while visitors are able to view the animals from above and below the water with the assistance of three large viewing windows. The pool itself is extremely large, being three metres at the deepest point, and containing approximately half a million litres of water. All this space and luxury—but Belfast only had one female Californian sea-lion to occupy it!

In order to rectify the situation, four captive-bred animals were located at Mystic Marine Aquarium in Connecticut, USA. In order to export these animals, the US Government had to grant its permission, which it would only do after the export request had been published in a Marine Mammals register and objections from anybody had been taken notice of. The placements officer at the Californian Marine Mammals Center duly noted Belfast's request, and decided to try his luck at solving the problem of the three blind sea-lions. He wrote to Belfast and suggested that it might like to consider taking their sea-lions as well.

After careful consideration, Belfast Zoo accepted the offer, and licences were applied for. However, the wheels of government turn very slowly. They took so long to complete a full circle that the three Californian sea-lions had sufficient time to become four! Arseno produced a beautiful, perfect female pup, fathered by Chariot, which was a total surprise to everybody! In honour of the pup's future home, she was named Belfast.

In May 1986, all four sea-lions arrived in Northern Ireland. They were transported by courtesy of the Flying Tigers, and were accompanied by three attendants. Initially, the new arrivals were kept to one side of the main enclosure, in order to acclimatise them to their new surroundings and to accustom the keepers to their needs.

Then the big day arrived. The sea-lions were released into their new enclosure. As they gingerly edged their sightless way down the beach to the water's edge, one could not begin to imagine what must have been going through their minds!

Belfast, whose vision was perfect, threw caution to the winds, plunged enthusiastically into the new pool, and immediately began playing with the other four young sea-lions who were already in residence. The remaining three waited cautiously until they had greeted the resident sea-lions. They all touched noses, a gesture of recognition and greeting. Only after this welcoming ceremony did the blind animals take the plunge.

After a few minutes of splashing and playing together, they carefully set off to explore the extent of their new environment. The zoo staff held their breath as they watched the astute animals begin their journey of exploration. With no vision, how would they know when they reached a wall or island? Their fears were quickly allayed, as the sea-lions expertly negotiated all obstacles. Such skill highlights the fact that sea-lions are able to utilise some other form of perception than sight. As they are able to dive to depths of many hundred feet below water in the wild, where it is totally dark, the possibility of some other sensory mechanism is likely.

It took just a few days for the newly established colony completely to settle down. There was the important matter of 'pecking order' to sort out, especially with the crucial issue of sleeping position at stake, but once the 'top dog' had been generally affirmed, the sea-lions lived peaceably together. Not that Chariot has been idle! Azul soon produced a large male pup. The birth was long and protracted and sadly her baby only lived for a few hours. Azul tried her best to revive the pup and spent several days searching for it, her maternal instincts being as strong, if not stronger, than the normally-sighted female. She is bound to have another pup eventually, and everyone hopes that this birth will be successful.

Without the help of the Californian Marine Mammals Center, and Belfast Zoo, Chariot, Azul and Arseno—not to mention Belfast—would not be alive today. As it is, they have continued to prosper and have made a valuable contribution to the world's captive-breeding programme. Eventually, Belfast Zoo intends to thank them by sending their offspring back into the wild!

KEN SIMS

What an Otter!

THRIGBY HALL WILDLIFE GARDENS

S atu and Sita are marvellous parents. Based at Thrigby Hall Wildlife Gardens near Great Yarmouth, this pair of tiny Malaysian short-clawed otters have produced many litters of cubs.

Like most zoo animals today, Satu and Sita were captive-bred and their cubs have, throughout the years, been moved to good homes in Britain and abroad. Finding homes for cubs from such good parentage never caused much of a problem—that is until Tigabelas came along.

The trouble was that Tigabelas, which means thirteen in Malay, was a bit of a rascal! He was Satu and Sita's thirteenth cub. Each had had a distinct and different personality of its own—but only Tigabelas had been so mischievous. He was different from his siblings, being sharper, bolder, and cheekier than the rest, and if a cub ever had to be scruffed and ignominiously returned to the nest, it was always Tigabelas. Could Ken Sims, in clear conscience, impose this bundle of trouble on someone else? He certainly could not keep the young otter, as he would soon rival his father and perhaps upset the successful breeding programme which had been established.

Inauspicious as his name might be, Tigabelas turned out to be rather lucky as, quite by chance, a superb new home was found for him. Ken had flown to Holland in order to attend the fourth World Conference on Breeding Endangered Species in Captivity. Co-sponsor of the event was Dick van Dam, who is the renowned director of Rotterdam Zoo. An informal conversation revealed that he had a particular interest in Asian animals and he immediately offered a home for Tigabelas at his zoo, despite Ken's explicit and detailed account of the young otter's 'peculiarities'.

Dick van Dam had successfully bred the same species of otter through several generations—many of them had lived in his family home. He felt that fresh blood, particularly that of such an obviously spirited male, would help enormously and he welcomed the opportunity to introduce Tigabelas to his new family.

Returning home to Norfolk, after a fascinating and productive conference, Ken felt satisfied, as he had not only learned a great deal and exchanged valuable information with fellow conservationists, but he had also settled the Tigabelas problem. Only one detail remained to be sorted out—how to get the otter to Rotterdam! Gone are the days of unrestricted animal transport, and previous escapes of otters in aircraft cabins had not encouraged the usually co-operative airlines to smile benignly upon the cuddly, but sharp-toothed, little charmers. As an alternative, Ken decided to use the Norfolk Line sea ferry that plied from Great Yarmouth to Scheveningen.

The helpfulness of the line's staff was only matched by their curiosity. The necessary documentation was thoroughly researched and the all-important EEC Blue CITES (Convention on International Trade in Endangered Species) document was issued by the Department of the Environment in Bristol. Understanding fully how the smallest error on such an important piece of paper could cause untoward trouble, the DOE very patiently checked every detail

Below: *Thrigby Hall has succeeded in breeding many litters of Malaysian small-clawed otters, which have been moved to good homes in Britain and abroad.*

on the morning of departure to ensure there could be no bureaucratic hiccups en route.

A professional escort service for Tigabelas was to be provided by Dr Richard Watling. Unfortunately, he turned up without his passport, and had to make an abrupt about turn and head back to Cambridge. Seven hours, several trains and numerous taxi miles later, he arrived back at the ship with his papers in order, only to discover that the otter's were not!

Tigabelas was sitting motionless in his VIP portable cabin, listening to the seemingly endless debate going on between Ken Sims and an intermediary who was relaying messages from some anonymous customs official. No matter how slowly, clearly and precisely Ken explained that the papers in his hand now replaced any need for the old Board of Trade export permits, the customs official did not, or perhaps would not, comprehend the situation.

The already desperate situation escalated by the hour. It was nearing midnight, so contact with either the Department of the Environment in Bristol or with a more informed customs man was out of the question. Tigabelas's luck was obviously changing and so was the direction of his journey—it looked like back to Thrigby for him!

Ken Sims could not bear the thought of the reception committee from Rotterdam Zoo waiting to greet the otter as the ferry arrived at dawn. There was no way to contact them. It was all very embarrassing, not to mention frustrating. Tigabelas did not think too highly of the evening's proceedings, either. He expressed his disgust in a typically Tigabelian manner—he escaped! As a rule, otters do not climb. Tigabelas was the exception. He scaled a vertical wall, two metres high, nosed his way up a roofing sheet and disappeared.

The chances of survival for an otter in the countryside near the Norfolk Broads are better than even. But Tigabelas was a foreigner in this terrain. The Broadland has to a great extent been spoilt even for the indigenous British otter—so what real chance did Tigabelas have? So the hunt was on! Long after Ken had felt inclined to bid Tigabelas a fond farewell, Richard Watling finally located the tiny, dark form of the otter, skulking in the undergrowth. A deft scoop with a net and Tigabelas was back among friends. All this—and the dawn was just breaking!

The morning brought a humble and an apologetic call from customs, explaining that although the CITES permit had been repeatedly explained to the officials, the information had somehow failed to permeate through to certain people! All the papers were correct, and the otter and his escort were free to depart. It sounded easier than it actually turned out to be, for the rearrangements took several weeks to complete. The day on which they finally boarded the ferry was bitterly cold, and as it chugged out of Great Yarmouth harbour to the sound of strange throbbing engines and the smell of diesel oil and Dutch gin, Ken and Dr Watling hoped that at long last Tigabelas would meet his Dutch girlfriend and so continue to improve already good Anglo-Dutch relations.

A Cat-alogue of Cat-astrophes

DARTMOOR WILDLIFE PARK

T he traffic warden lay flat on his back on the pavement, watched over by an extremely puzzled Siberian tiger called Topaz and his equally bemused handler, Lynne Daw. As the man slowly came round, Lynne asked, 'What's wrong? I told you that the tiger had arrived!'

'But I thought you meant that one,' he replied, pointing up at the carved wooden tiger which adorns the roof of Dartmoor Wildlife Park's transit van.

Lynne had been asked to take her hand-reared Siberian tiger, Topaz, to the cinema to watch *The Beastmaster*, which a local newspaper thought would provide a very entertaining story and photograph. She had got permission to park her vehicle right outside the cinema, as Topaz, although tame, did not like being surrounded by the crowds which he inevitably attracted. She duly pulled up in the strictly 'No Parking' area, and, on cue, the traffic warden strolled over. 'So this is the tiger I've been asked to look out for,' he had said.

'Of course,' replied Lynne, emerging from the back of the vehicle with Topaz. One glimpse of the enormous tiger and the warden passed out cold! Lynne could hardly believe her eyes. Topaz, who was about eleven months old, was just another of her babies, and she did not dream that the sight of her much-loved youngster would scare anyone—let alone cause a full-grown traffic warden to faint! It is quite amazing how Lynne, who is barely 5 ft 1 in. tall, can control and communicate with the enormous cats, while taller, stronger males flinch at the mere sight of them.

Lynne has hand-reared many of the cats at the wildlife park she runs in Devon with her husband Ellis. The most recent was a jaguar cub, who was so amazing that she was named Grace. Grace was one of three jaguars born in December 1986. Sadly, two did not survive, and Grace had to be retrieved from her mother and reared by Lynne.

Lynne had to sleep on the couch for three months while she fed Grace, whose demand for food was seemingly endless. Grace developed a lot more quickly than the tiger cubs Lynne was more used to rearing, and soon managed to climb out of her box and explore the house. Lynne learned of Grace's adventurous spirit one night when, feeling totally exhausted, she inadvertently fell asleep.

Grace woke, hungry as ever, and when she failed to rouse Lynne with her wailing, clambered out of her box, negotiated the settee, and sunk her teeth into sleeping Lynne's nose! With a jaguar hanging on your nose, it is impossible for anyone to doze! Grace, unlike the tiger cubs, grew very attached to her toys. She slept with a teddy bear and rabbit, which she would not allow anyone else to touch. The absolute centre of Grace's affections, however, was an old blanket which, no matter how dirty and smelly it was, she simply would not allow anyone to tamper with! Indeed, Lynne gave up trying, preferring to explain the reason for the unusual aroma coming from Grace's corner, rather than attempt to wash the precious blanket.

Grace did have a minor flirtation with a hessian sack, however, transferring all her affections to the brown, rough material. When the owner of the sack finally decided to retrieve his property, he had no conception of how possessive the apparently sweet and cuddly 'kitten' could be. He quickly learned! As he reached to take it, Grace pounced and attacked him with all the venom she could muster, which, despite her size, was considerable! She was so angry and her tantrum so ferocious, that eventually, Ellis Daw had to place a box over her in the hope that she would calm down. A few minutes later, when Lynne lifted the box, Grace was, indeed, quieter, but certainly unrepentant, and she expressed her disgust by sulking for hours!

Grace used to follow Lynne around the zoo while she worked but, having become aware of Grace's tendency suddenly to develop an inexplicable passion for some object, Lynne kept a very keen eye on the young jaguar's activities. However, the desire to possess a visitor's bright green, woolly scarf was just too intense for Lynne to combat. Grace simply attacked it and hung grimly on to one end of the alluring article. 'I managed to persuade the lady to unravel the scarf from around her neck. Grace was tugging as hard as she could, and I could envisage the poor lady going blue in the face as the scarf tightened around her neck,' recalled Lynne. 'The visitor thought Grace couldn't hurt her as she was only playing, which was true—but she didn't realise just how hard Grace could play, and I did!'

Lynne grabbed one end of the scarf while Grace clung grimly to the other. She would not even swap it for her beloved blanket! Only when the visitor bent forward to help and Grace pounced on her matching woolly hat did Grace drop her end of the scarf! 'She ran off with this woolly hat in her mouth and I didn't know what to do. At first it looked as though she was going to take it into the water tank to play with—but, thankfully, she changed her mind. She was chewing and gnawing it so much, I was just waiting for the lady to demand payment for the destruction of her clothes! Finally I had to tap the end of Grace's nose before she would drop it, and then move like greased lightning, as she only released the mangled hat for a split second.

'The visitor, thankfully, was incredibly kind. In fact, she was rather proud of her jaguar-chewed hat and said she couldn't wait to tell her friends, who wouldn't believe that a jaguar was responsible for the damage!'

Grace eventually had to be returned to the park, which caused heartbreak for both Lynne and the young jaguar. Both cried through the night.

Grace, like the tigers and lions, has never forgotten Lynne. As Lynne walks around the enclosures, the powerful cats turn into purring kittens at the sound of her voice or the sight of her approach. The obvious and deep affection between the tiny woman and the enormous cats is quite remarkable, and it is obvious that Lynne adores and is adored by her very special babies.

Below: *Jaguars at Dartmoor Wildlife Park.*

Zoo Addresses

Banham Zoo Ltd: The Grove, Banham, Norwich NR16 2HB

Blackpool Municipal Zoological Gardens: East Drive, Blackpool, Lancs FY3 8PP

Bristol, Clifton & West of England Zoological Society: Bristol BS8 3HA

Chessington World of Adventure: Chessington, Surrey KT9 2NE

City of Belfast Zoo: Hazlewood, Antrim Road, Belfast BT36 7PN

Colchester Zoo: Maldon Road, Stanway, Essex CO3 5SL

Dartmoor Wildlife Park: Sparkwell, Plymouth, Devon PL7 5DG

Drusilla's Zoo Park: Alfriston, East Sussex BN26 5QS

Gatwick Zoo and Aviaries: Russ Hill, Charlwood, Surrey R86 0EG

Jersey Wildlife Preservation Trust: Les Augres Manor, Trinity, Jersey, Channel Islands

Kilverstone Wildlife Park: Thetford, Norfolk LP24 2RL

Knowsley Safari Park: Prescot, Merseyside L34 4AN

Linton Zoological Gardens: Hadstock Road, Linton, Cambs CB1 6NT

Manor House Wildlife and Leisure Park: St Florence, Tenby, Dyfed, South Wales SR70 8RJ

Marwell Zoological Park: Golden Common, Nr Winchester, Hants SO21 1JH

Mole Hall Wildlife Park: Widdington, Newport, Essex CB11 3SS

The North of England Zoological Society: Upton-by-Chester, Cheshire CH2 1LD

Padstow Bird Gardens: Padstow, Cornwall PL28 8BB

Robin Hill Country Parks Ltd: Combley Farm, Downend, Newport, Isle of Wight

The Royal Zoological Society of Scotland: Murrayfield, Edinburgh EH12 6TS

Southport Zoo: Princes Park, Southport, Merseyside PR8 1RX

Stagsden Bird Gardens: Stagsden, Bedfordshire MK43 8SL

Thrigby Hall Wildlife Gardens: Filby, Great Yarmouth, Norfolk NR29 3DS

The Tropical Bird Gardens: Rode, Nr Bath, Somerset BA3 6QW

Windsor Safari Park Ltd: Winkfield Road, Windsor, Berks SL4 4AY

Zoo Park (Twycross) Ltd: Norton-juxta-Twycross, Atherstone, Warwicks CV9 3PX

The Zoological Society of Glasgow and West of Scotland: Uddingston, Glasgow G71 7RZ

The Zoological Society of London: Regent's Park, London NW1 4RY

The Zoological Society of Wales: Colwyn Bay, Clwyd, North Wales LL28 5UY